Center Yourself with God

A Mindful
MOMENT

5-Minute Meditations
and Devotions

DR. IRENE KRAEGEL

ZONDERKIDZ

A Mindful Moment
Copyright © 2022 by Zondervan

Requests for information should be addressed to:
Zonderkidz, *3900 Sparks Dr. SE, Grand Rapids, Michigan 49546*

ISBN 978-0-310-77766-3 (hardcover)
ISBN 978-0-310-79015-0 (audio)
ISBN 978-0-310-77819-6 (ebook)

Library of Congress Cataloging-in-Publication Data

Names: Kraegel, Irene, author.
Title: A mindful moment: 5-minute meditations and devotions / Irene Bess Kraegel.
Description: Grand Rapids: Zondervan, 2022. | Audience: Ages 13 and up |
Summary: "A Mindful Moment focuses on four key categories-physical sensations,
    negative emotions, compassion to self, and lovingkindness to others. It can be used
    as a guide for daily meditation and reflection but allows for flexibility, providing
    inspiration and God's peace in any situation. Use it on your journey to self-love and
    then let it take you to a place of love for all as Jesus calls us to love"—Provided by
    publisher.
Identifiers: LCCN 2022003344 (print) | LCCN 2022003345 (ebook) | ISBN 9780310777663
    (hardcover) | ISBN 9780310778196 (ebook)
Subjects: LCSH: Meditation—Christianity. | Mindfulness (Psychology) | Meditations.
Classification: LCC BV4813 .K73 2022 (print) | LCC BV4813 (ebook) | DDC 248.3/4—dc23/
    eng/20220301
LC record available at https://lccn.loc.gov/2022003344
LC ebook record available at https://lccn.loc.gov/2022003345

Written by Dr. Irene Kraegel
Cover Design: Diane Mielke
Interior Design: Denise Froehlich

Printed in the United States of America

22 23 24 25 26   LSC   10 9 8 7 6 5 4 3 2 1

Contents

Introduction

    What is Meditation?....................................5

    Why Meditate? 6

    Brief History of Christian Meditation Practices.........7

    How-to Guide for Simple Meditation...................8

    How to Use This Book.............................. 10

Devotions

    150 Devotions 14–163

Meditation Guides

    Meditation Guides Introduction 164–165

    Body Scan.. 166

    Sitting Practice..................................... 167

    Walking/Wheeling Meditation...................168–169

    Stretching/Yoga Meditation..................... 170–171

    Lovingkindness/Blessing Practice 172–173

    Mountain Meditation...........................174–175

    Breathing Space............................... 176–177

    Working with Difficulty Meditation 178–179

    Sensing Meditation............................180–181

    Eating Meditation 182–183

    Centering Prayer 184–185

FAQ: the Nuts and Bolts of Meditation

Dedicated to Tim, Ellen, Caleb, Ethan, Laurel, Amelia, Charis, Doug, Milo, Ted, Tom, & Emmett, with all my love.

Introduction

You've heard of meditation, and maybe you've even tried it out yourself. But what exactly is meditation?

I've been practicing mindfulness meditation for several years, teaching it at a Christian university, and sharing it with clients through my psychology practice, and here's my definition: Meditation is taking time to focus your attention on a particular thing, and pulling your attention back to that thing over and over whenever your focus wanders. And choosing that "particular thing" to focus on is up to you! Meditation is a very broad concept and also a very simple one. But it's a powerful practice for Christian teens who want to cultivate mental health, live with compassion, and walk in step with God.

In this book, we'll be exploring a particular type of meditation practice called mindfulness. Mindfulness involves focusing our attention *on the present moment* (over and over), and doing that with an attitude of compassion, openness toward what is new, and non-judgment. If these words sound familiar, it might be because you've also heard them referenced in the Bible! God calls us to live compassionately, be open to new things the Spirit is teaching, and move from judgment to grace.

Practicing mindfulness can include "formal practices" like sitting (or laying) in silence, moving your body in a deliberate way, extending love toward others through guided thoughts, or tuning into your senses (ever tried an eating meditation?). It can also include "informal practices" like drawing your attention to what is present in any moment during the day, with a particular focus on getting out of your head and into your body. We'll be trying out both formal and informal mindfulness practices in this devotional, and we'll be doing it all with an awareness of God's presence along the way.

· · · · · · · · · · · · · · ## Why Meditate? · · · · · · · · · · · · · · ·

You may have heard the expression "all truth is God's truth." This means that we can explore any part of God's world—any topic—and in the process we can learn about God because God created all things (Col. 1:16). So whether or not something has a "Christian" label on it, it could be used by God. Everything from medical treatments to architecture to fitness classes are gifts for our benefit, and people often benefit from these gifts even if they don't recognize God as the giver. As an example, people who brush their teeth will have better dental hygiene, whether or not they thank God for the gift of the modern toothbrush. But as Christians, how cool to also have the opportunity to thank the giver!

This is true of mindfulness too—it is a secular, research-based approach to mental health that is also based on ancient traditions, and it provides benefit whether or not we recognize God along the way. But Christians can include an awareness of God as they use this mental health tool of mindfulness meditation. In this way, the practice of Christian mindfulness can help you meet God and deepen your spiritual walk.

The meditation practices in this book are drawn from a modern tradition of mindfulness called Mindfulness-Based Stress

Reduction (MBSR), created in the 1970s at the University of Massachusetts Medical School. Numerous studies on MBSR have identified the following benefits for people who practice regularly:

- Decreased anxiety, fewer recurrences of depression, and better stress reduction
- Increased feelings of connection with others
- Improved physical health

The meditation practices in this devotional will be rooted in both science and Scripture. You will have the opportunity to meditate as you pray, move your body, sit still, and engage in other activities. In the process, you'll learn which types of mindfulness meditation are the most supportive of your faith and your mental wellbeing.

Brief History of Christian Meditation Practices

God-followers have been using silent meditation throughout history to meet God. In the Old Testament, we are reminded to "Be still, and know that I am God" (Psalm 46:10). In the New Testament, Jesus sets an example repeatedly of withdrawing to a quiet place to pray. Since the time of Christ, there are many ways the Christian community has used meditation and contemplation to connect with God. Here is a sampling of a few well-known examples:

- About 200 years after Christ, many people moved into the desert to practice being present with God. We call

this group the Desert Fathers and Desert Mothers. They
believed that learning to be silent and to control thoughts
was a way of caring for their souls.

- In the 1500s, St. Ignatius started an order of monks called
the Jesuits. This group still exists, and has a focus on
seeing God in the everyday, moment-to-moment elements
of daily life.
- In the 1960s, Centering Prayer was developed as a method
of meditation with a focus on God's presence in the
present moment.
- An ancient method of meditation called Lectio Divina
invites participants to hear a Scripture meditation multiple
times and dwell on the passage in a variety of ways, listening
for what God might have to say in the present moment.
- Taizé worship is a contemplative way of worship which
includes silence and corporate meditation.

While some Christian traditions place a higher value on
silence than others, Christians throughout history have known
that listening to God is part of developing our faith. And if we
want to listen to God, we have to learn to be quiet and pay attention. Mindfulness meditation is a way of learning to pay attention,
and it is a tool available to Christians who want to deepen their
relationship with God and stay mentally healthy at the same time.

····· **How-to Guide for Simple Meditation** ·····

You'll get the most out of this devotional if you take the time to
try out the mindfulness practices that go along with it, and you'll

find a lot of different kinds to try (both formal and informal). Meditation isn't easy, but the guidelines are pretty simple.

- Don't expect to concentrate perfectly. Your mind will wander a lot and that's okay—it's part of meditation practice. Whenever you notice you're distracted, you can congratulate yourself for noticing and return back to the focus of your meditation.
- Try out different postures. If you like sitting upright, go for it! If you prefer to lie down or stand up or even move around, you are welcome to experiment with those postures as well. You can also keep your eyes open or closed, whatever works best for you. If there is an instruction in a meditation that is difficult for you, you might try it out and then change it if needed.
- Practice being kind to yourself as you meditate! God loves you and provides grace for all of your weaknesses, and you can practice doing the same. Receiving and practicing God's compassion is the goal.
- Give up any expectations for meditation. You're not trying to feel more calm, relaxed, or happy. The goal is simply to practice keeping your mind on whatever is happening in the moment, and doing that over and over whenever your mind wanders. This will pay off in the long run, even if you're not sure of the point at first.

You'll find instructions for a few standard, formal mindfulness meditations in this book, such as the body scan, sitting practice, walking/wheeling meditation, and lovingkindness/

blessing practice. These are practices you may want to use on a regular basis, coming back to them daily or weekly. You'll also find instructions for more informal mindfulness practices that you can implement in your daily life as you work through the devotionals.

This book has 150 different devotionals, each with a Bible verse and a meditation practice to go with it. You can read the devotions straight through or mix up the order. You can read them each once or repeat the ones you like over and over. Whatever floats your boat!

Each devotional will be accompanied by a meditation practice. Some of these are formal mindfulness practices adapted from the Mindfulness-Based Stress Reduction (MBSR) tradition:

- Body scan—notice sensations in each part of your body
- Sitting practice—notice breathing, as well as physical sensations, thoughts, feelings, and behaviors/urges
- Walking/wheeling meditation—notice your movement through space as you walk or roll a wheelchair
- Stretching/yoga meditation—notice your mind and body interacting with one another as you move your muscles
- Lovingkindness/blessing practice—receive and extend compassion
- Mountain meditation—connect with your stability in the midst of constant change
- Breathing space—notice how you are doing overall

- Working with difficulty—acknowledge and care for any challenges you are experiencing
- Sensing meditation—focus on one of your body's senses
- Eating meditation—experience your food with full awareness
- Centering prayer—notice God's presence

You will find guides for these formal practices in the back of the book (with symbols helping you match them up quickly with each devotional), and they are meant to be used in as little as three minutes. If you have time and interest, feel free to extend them longer for greater benefit. Most mindfulness practitioners find that 10–20 minutes is the ideal amount of time for a formal practice, and these longer practices can be especially helpful when your uncomfortable emotions are intense.

The informal mindfulness practices in this book are described at the end of the devotionals and don't require any additional instructions. Keep an eye out for those as you read along.

· · · · · · · · · · · · · · · Going Deeper · · · · · · · · · · · · · · · ·

One great way to make the most out of your Christian mindfulness practice is by using a journal for written reflection. Each devotional will give you specific instructions on how to do that if you choose. When writing observations about your mindfulness experiences, the following Noticing Guide can help you out! In fact, you might want to keep this page dog-eared so you can find the Noticing Guide below easily.

During my meditation practice, I noticed the following:

Physical sensations *(what I felt in my body)*
Thoughts *(what went through my mind)*
Feelings *(what emotions I felt)*
Behaviors & urges *(what I did or wanted to do)*
Spiritual awareness *(what I noticed about God)*

There is no "right or wrong" observation when you practice mindfulness, so anything you write will be fine! It's just a chance to practice pausing and noticing. Keeping your written reflections in one place will also help you go back later to review and remember what God is bringing to your attention through your mindfulness practice.

·············· **Getting Support** ··············

Practicing mindfulness gets us in touch with *all* of our emotions more directly, even those that are uncomfortable. While that's part of the healing process, it can also feel confusing or overwhelming at times. If you have any questions about troubling thoughts and emotions in the course of your Christian mindfulness meditations, don't be afraid to talk those through with a trusted adult. You were not meant to walk this road alone, and many people are eager to share this journey with you (whether you've met them yet or not).

There are some thoughts and feelings that you should always get support talking through—suicidal thoughts, traumatic memories, losing touch with reality, and urges to use drugs or alcohol are all indications that it's time to reach out. Fortunately, symptoms such as these are treatable, and help is available.

Wondering who you can trust? Consider people who are good listeners, slow to judgment, wise in their advice, and good role models. This could include older family members (like parents, grandparents, or other guardians), pastors, teachers, coaches, doctors, school guidance counselors, and mental health counselors. You might also have some wise peers that you have come to trust with the more difficult parts of your story. If you're feeling unsafe and are unsure if there is anyone you can trust, reach out to the National Suicide Prevention Lifeline (800-273-8255) for support and direction—they can help you brainstorm your next steps for getting help.

God did not make us to figure everything out alone—he put us in community. Allow your community to support you as you learn and grow!

Devotion 1

My flesh and my heart may fail,
but God is the strength of my heart
and my portion forever.

PSALM 73:26

You've had days when you felt discouraged, when you didn't perform as well as you hoped, or when you felt drained. Days when you hit a wall and you weren't sure you had it in you to keep going. Days when your "flesh and heart failed."

Maybe you've even had weeks, or months, or years like this. It's no secret that life can be hard. The struggle is real.

Fortunately, God restores us when we're having a hard time. We can't expect to feel our best all the time, but we *can* expect that God will get us what we need. Over time, we learn to pay attention to the mechanisms God has created for our strengthening. We get better at noticing what helps us to feel better and then using those tools. Kind of like when we learn to notice how to fill up a car's gas tank when it's empty, we also learn how to help ourselves feel better so that we can be strengthened in our hearts and receive the "portion" that God promises us during hard times.

Practice Make a list (perhaps in your journal) of things you do when life is tough and you need restrengthening. For example, some teens use exercise, prayer, music, journaling, or talking with friends as ways to get emotionally grounded. This list of God-given coping skills will be important for you as you move through the meditations in this book.

Devotion 2

"Be still, and know that I am God;/ I will be exalted among the nations,/ I will be exalted in the earth."

PSALM 46:10

Boredom can be the worst, and most of us avoid it like the plague. So why would you want to sit quietly without any distraction? What could God possibly be thinking in asking you just to sit still and meditate?

It turns out that avoiding boredom is often just a defense mechanism against the uncomfortable feelings and thoughts that we need to deal with. Stillness helps you notice those feelings and thoughts while providing an opportunity to notice God's presence too. God has the healing and strength you need, but you have to get quiet so that you can notice and receive that provision.

What have past experiences with silence been like for you? Whether or not it's comfortable, being still is one of the ways that we show up for God and allow God to show up for us.

Practice Take three minutes to just sit in stillness. During that time, stay quiet (maybe with closed eyes) and pay attention to the experiences in your body and mind. Notice that God is present with you. You don't have to feel a certain way. You're just noticing what happens when you sit still. When you are finished, jot down some observations in your journal using the Noticing Guide on page 12 for guidance.

Devotion 3

Do you not know that your bodies are temples of the Holy Spirit, who is in you, whom you have received from God?

1 CORINTHIANS 6:19

A temple is an awesome place! It's created to be a beautiful home for God to dwell, and it inspires worship in people who pass through. People travel the world to see temples.

God's Word says that your body is a temple where the Holy Spirit dwells. This physical body of yours houses God's divine spirit. Wow! This means that by definition, your body is beautiful and awe-inducing. It's made to spend time in, and it's a great place to hang out if you want to meet God. Like all temples, your body also includes clues about the God who dwells there. This is the case whether or not you like your body in a given moment.

One of the hallmark practices of mindfulness meditation is called the body scan. This practice will move you through each part of your body to help you pay attention to whatever is there. Whether or not you notice God along the way, you can be assured that this "temple of the Holy Spirit" houses God's divine presence and reflects God's awesomeness. We can learn about ourselves and our Creator by paying attention to our bodies.

 Practice Following the body scan guide on page 166, allow yourself to spend time paying attention to your body which is a "temple of the Holy Spirit." Notice that God dwells here with you. When you are finished, jot down some observations in your journal.

Grace and peace to you from God our
Father and the Lord Jesus Christ.

2 CORINTHIANS 1:2

We live each day only because of God's grace. Breath demonstrates that. Each time we take a breath, we are receiving a gift from God. We cannot manufacture or control our breath. We can simply receive it as grace in each moment that we are alive.

For many people, breath can also be a pathway to God's peace. Breathing has a rhythm to it, and it can be calming to focus on the breath without trying to control it. If you pay attention to your breathing, you might notice the following physical sensations:

- Changing temperatures under your nose
- Gentle lift and fall of your shoulders
- Belly moving in and out with the diaphragm
- Lungs in your chest contracting and expanding
- Slight pause between the in-breaths and out-breaths

These are just a few of the many sensations occurring with each breath! Whatever you notice, God's grace and peace is offered with each breath—gifts from our Creator. Learning to notice your breathing is one way to receive God's grace and peace!

 Practice Following the sitting practice guide on page 167, take a few minutes to pay attention to your breathing, noticing that you are in God's presence. When you are finished, jot down some observations in your journal.

Devotion 5

"Come to me, all you who are weary and burdened, and I will give you rest. Take my yoke upon you and learn from me, for I am gentle and humble in heart, and you will find rest for your souls. For my yoke is easy and my burden is light."

MATTHEW 11:28–30

Sometimes we need to set things down simply because they are heavy. But how often do we expect ourselves to keep holding on to heavy things out of guilt or spite or a need to prove ourselves? Maybe the heavy thing is a self-critical thought or a hurtful relationship or an insistence on doing something perfectly. These types of heavy things hurt us when we carry them for too long, and they are worth putting down. Just like setting down a really heavy box, there can be a lot of relief in letting go of something that is causing us harm because it is too heavy.

Jesus himself encourages us to put down our heavy burdens, and promises to exchange them for something lighter. When you feel the weight of the world on your shoulders, it could be helpful to pause and ask yourself—could I give up some of this heavy burden? Is it possible that Jesus has something lighter for me to carry, something easier? How could I rest in this moment?

Practice Following the breathing space guide on page 176–177, pay particular attention to any parts of your body that are holding tension. Notice if that tension is useful. If not, consider letting it go. When you are finished, jot down some observations in your journal.

Devotion 6

A furious squall came up, and the waves broke over the boat, so that it was nearly swamped. Jesus was in the stern, sleeping on a cushion. The disciples woke him and said to him, "Teacher, don't you care if we drown?"

MARK 4:37–38

It certainly seemed logical for Jesus' disciples to panic when their boat was being overwhelmed by a storm, filling up with water that threatened to sink them.

But Jesus was sleeping through it all, and was completed unpanicked. When the disciples woke him up in their anxiety and anger, accusing him of not caring, he told the sea to be still (an order it obeyed) and then asked them, perplexed, "Why are you afraid? Have you still no faith?"

It's been said that we can't stop the storms in life but we can learn to sail. We can learn to notice when our panicking is not helping stop the storm, notice that God is calm, and be open to the expectation that Jesus will bring peace once again.

Practice Following the working with difficulty guide on page 178–179, practice noticing any "storms" that might be present for you. Notice any tendency to panic in response, and maybe smile at yourself with compassion (it's normal!). Notice that Jesus is with you in the boat and be curious about how the waves might change over time as you ride out the storm with your non-panicked God. When you are finished, jot down some observations in your journal.

Devotion 7

Jesus declared, "I am the bread of life. Whoever comes to me will never go hungry, and whoever believes in me will never be thirsty."

JOHN 6:35

God is really into metaphors, and food is a big one. Jesus compares himself, in fact, to bread. He says that when we come to him, he makes us full. We have the sustenance that we need.

It's pretty cool to think about God as food because most of us like food quite a bit. It often tastes good, it's fun to eat, and it gives us satisfaction. So Jesus is reminding us that hanging out with him is something really great, just like eating food.

By paying attention to eating, we can learn more about Jesus filling us up. A mindful eating exercise can help us tune into our experience of eating. It helps us notice the gift of food, and helps us tune into our creator God. It helps us receive food with gratitude. It also teaches us about this experience of being fed, in a way that can help us understand the experience of Jesus being our "bread of life." With God, we always have the opportunity to be filled up again.

Practice Following the eating meditation guide on page 182–183, find something to eat and choose a quiet place to engage in some brief mindful eating. Be conscious of receiving this "fuel" from God that fills you up. When you are finished, jot down some observations in your journal.

Devotion 8

How lovely is your dwelling place,
Lord Almighty!

PSALM 84:1

Teens can be really hard on themselves, and so can adults, especially when it comes to our bodies. We think we are too tall or short, too fat or skinny, too light or dark. We might be able to acknowledge one part of our body as okay, but have trouble accepting another part. This type of self-criticism creates a lot of emotional pain and distracts us from the truth of our own beauty.

Scripture describes you as a dwelling place for God, a temple. Jesus points out (John 15) that God abides (lives) in us as we also abide in God. This suggests that your body is not meant to be judged, criticized, and changed, but instead you are a dwelling place for God. God loves to be with you, and he loves the way he made you.

How do you typically see your body? Your size, shape, and color are just right for God, a "lovely" dwelling place for the divine. With practice, you may find that your body can seem just right for you too.

Practice Following the body scan guide on page 166, practice observing your body with wonder as a place that God dwells. See if it is possible to lift judgments of your body's size, shape, color, or other features, simply observing this cool dwelling place for God as it was made to be. When you are finished, jot down some observations in your journal.

Devotion 9

"I will rain down bread from heaven for you. The people are to go out each day and gather enough for that day. In this way I will test them and see whether they will follow my instructions."

EXODUS 16:4

How much of your mental space is taken up with worries about the future? Maybe it's wondering how a game will turn out or what grade you'll get. Some worries are small and others big.

One way to take care of your mental health is to practice bringing attention from worries about the future back to the present moment. When the Israelites escaped from Egypt into the wilderness and worried they would die of hunger, this is how God instructed them to learn trust in God—focus on the food (the manna) provided TODAY. Trying to hoard manna for tomorrow would not work. They had to just gather enough for that day and trust that God would provide what was needed the next day.

You will always have what you need for today. Not for tomorrow (you don't need that yet), not for yesterday (you don't need that anymore), but for today. Like the Israelites, God encourages us to gather what we need from his provision each day and trust his provision for tomorrow.

Practice Following the sitting practice guide on page 167, notice how God is providing the breath you need for right now. You don't have the next breath yet, but you will in the moment that you need it. God provides. When you are finished, jot down some observations in your journal.

Devotion 10

Even though I walk/ through the darkest valley,/
I will fear no evil,/ for you are with me;/ your
rod and your staff,/ they comfort me.

PSALM 23:4

How do you move your body? Perhaps you walk on two feet, perhaps you turn the wheels of a chair. How much attention do you pay to the movements that allow for this change of location?

Walking or rolling a wheelchair are just two examples of movements that we often take for granted. Moving involves a complicated coordination of muscles, brain waves, balance, sensation, control, etc. God equips you for this movement in ways that you may not even be noticing. When you walk or wheel, you're likely to be rehashing stories about the past, predictions about the future, or everything EXCEPT the miracle of moving through space. But walking and other movements are everyday miracles!

God is with you—through the dark valleys, through the fears, you are guided and comforted. You won't get stuck in the dark, you will continue to experience change and move forward. Are you paying attention?

Practice Following the walking/wheeling meditation guide on pages 168–169, take time to get out of your head and into your body as you appreciate whatever way God has provided for you to move through space. Notice that God is with you through each part of that journey. When you are finished, jot down some observations in your journal.

Devotion 11

Mount Sinai was covered with smoke, because the LORD descended on it in fire. . . . As the sound of the trumpet grew louder and louder, Moses spoke and the voice of God answered him [with thunder].

EXODUS 19:18–19

Mountains are strong and stable, unmovable and unchangeable. Or are they? We know they are big and solid, but the reality is that mountains are in a constant state of flux. Every day, they experience slight shifting. Sometimes lightning or earthquakes or volcanoes create additional change. And occasionally, God adds extra excitement, like when he descended on Mt. Sinai with fire and smoke and spoke to Moses in thunder.

Change is often hard for humans. We like to think that our lives are always strong and stable. But we are a lot like mountains. We are firmly rooted while also being in a constant state of flux. And sometimes God adds a little fire and smoke and talking thunder—extra excitement that we're not sure what to do with.

But mountains remain stable even through all of the changes, moment to moment, and you also have a rooted stability that remains even through all of the changes. You are like a mountain.

Practice Following the mountain meditation guide on page 174–175, practice noticing how you are stable but also in constant flux. See if it's possible to be open to both your rootedness and your moment-to-moment changes, knowing that God gives you what you need just like a mountain. When you are finished, jot down some observations in your journal.

Devotion 12

The LORD your God is with you, the Mighty Warrior
who saves. He will take great delight in you; in his
love he will ... rejoice over you with singing."

ZEPHANIAH 3:17

God delights in you. He loves you and rejoices over you. Other translations say that he renews you and that he rests in quiet love for you. When we are quiet and care for ourselves, it is a way of receiving the love, delight, and renewal that God has for us.

There are many ways we can be renewed in our minds and bodies, and these are given to us by God. Many types of renewal are related to physical movement. Even something as simple as stretching can be used by God for renewing our minds and bodies. Taking a moment to stretch our arms and legs can be deeply renewing and help us continue on with new energy.

When you take time for gentle movement, as you feel the refreshment and renewal, you might want to imagine this as being renewed by God's love. God rejoices over you and is glad about you. God loves you and invites you to take time to pause, celebrate, get quiet, and be renewed by him.

Practice Following the stretching/yoga guide on page 170–171, recognize that the renewal of your muscles through stretching is one of the ways God renews you. As much as you are able, be conscious of receiving God's love, gladness, and renewal as you move your body. When you are finished, jot down some observations in your journal.

Devotion 13

Let us lift up our hearts and our hands to God in heaven . . .

LAMENTATIONS 3:41

In many church traditions, there is a part of liturgy when the leader says "Lift up your hearts," and the congregation responds "We lift them up to the Lord." This idea of "lifting up" shows up in Scripture for lifting up our hands, our eyes, our voices, our prayers, and our souls to God. There is also reference to bowing down—bowing our heads, knees, and whole bodies in worship.

Can you picture this literally for a minute, people moving like this in church? Whether your church's worship style is all about movement or you're better known as the "frozen chosen," it may bring up a new image of people lifting their hearts and bowing their knees during worship. And it seems that this type of physical expression of worship brings delight to God.

Interestingly, moving like this is also good for our bodies and minds. It strengthens us physically and mentally. And when we incorporate an awareness of God's presence, we can also utilize the movement of exercise to worship God—to lift up our hearts and bow our heads to God, our maker.

Practice Following the stretching/yoga guide on page 170–171, notice the opportunity to be present to your body in the moment as you move. In lifting and bowing, you are cultivating your health while also taking the opportunity to worship God with your physical movements. When you are finished, jot down some observations in your journal.

Devotion 14

... as God's chosen people, holy and dearly loved,
clothe yourselves with compassion, kindness,
humility, gentleness and patience.

COLOSSIANS 3:12

When you get dressed in the morning, you probably put on some clothes, shoes, maybe a jacket ... Whatever is needed for the weather and the occasion that day, you prepare by clothing yourself.

Here's something else to put on: compassion. Imagine if we started the day by clothing ourselves with compassion. This implies we are ready with compassion for other people, but that our compassion for others starts with compassion for ourselves.

It's not always easy to have compassion for ourselves. Sometimes it comes more easily for others, especially those who seem vulnerable. Imagine a scared child or puppy. You might naturally want to reach out and comfort them. So if it's hard to show compassion toward yourself, one place to start is to imagine yourself as a small child. Each of us needs care, kindness, and compassion. Along with your other clothing, you might try on some compassion for yourself today as well.

Practice Following the lovingkindness/blessing guide on page 172–173, choose yourself as the focus for this meditation. Practice "wearing" compassion as you extend a blessing toward yourself, which equips you to extend compassion more effectively to others over time. When you are finished, write a brief prayer of response in your journal.

Devotion 15

I have learned to be content whatever the circumstances. I know what it is to be in need, and I know what it is to have plenty. . . . I can do all this through him who gives me strength.

PHILIPPIANS 4:11–13

When you fantasize about your life being better, what is it that you imagine? We can always think of something—more money, nicer stuff, cooler friends, a different body, cheerier feelings.

The book of Philippians in the Bible was written by the Apostle Paul, who endured all kinds of suffering during his life—hunger, beatings, shipwrecks, robberies, imprisonment, and abandonment, to name just a few. And yet he is the one who wrote these words about learning to be content (through God's strength).

Most of us are much more skilled at complaining than we are at contentment. But what if you have enough right now? God is faithful in giving us what we need when we need it. Grasping for more simply gives us practice in grasping for more, and we are seldom satisfied when we get what we think we've been wanting. God encourages us to practice noticing and receiving what we already have with open hands.

Practice Following the sitting practice guide on page 167, notice ways your mind moves to how you want things to be different. See if it's possible to cultivate a spirit of acceptance and contentment in response to what is here, noticing that God is giving you everything you need. When you are finished, jot down some observations in your journal.

Devotion 16

Let the heavens rejoice, let the earth be glad;/ let the sea resound, and all that is in it./ Let the fields be jubilant, and everything in them;/ let all the trees of the forest sing for joy./ Let all creation rejoice before the Lord ...

PSALM 96:11–13

The world is full of sound. Depending on where you are, you might hear vehicles, voices, music, nature ... Most of the sounds around us do not register in our consciousness—we can't possibly process them all at once.

So what happens when you sit still and focus on sounds for a while? (Or if sound is not available to you, when you focus on your own way of physically perceiving the world?) You may start to become aware of sounds you didn't notice before such as leaves rustling, birds singing, maybe even your own breath. If you live by an ocean, perhaps you'll hear "the sea roar." Depending on where you live you may even hear sounds mentioned in this Psalm.

Sounds of the earth remind us that we are part of nature, this world that God has made. When we pay attention, sounds also remind us that the earth is "rejoicing" and "exulting" before God. Hearing provides one way of tuning in to the party.

Practice Following the sensing guide on page 180–181, practice tuning in to your sense of hearing by listening to sounds. Notice sounds from inside the room, from outside the room, and perhaps even from your own body. When you are finished, jot down some observations in your journal.

Devotion 17

Blind Pharisee! First clean the inside of the cup and dish, and then the outside also will be clean.

MATTHEW 23:26

Jesus reserved his harshest words for fake people. He didn't like it when people pretended to have it all together, especially when they mixed that better-than-thou attitude with religion. He wanted the Pharisees (religious leaders) and others to admit their problems with humility. He made a point of hanging out with people who were sick, struggling, and messing things up big time.

In some ways this is good news, because we're all sick, struggling, and messing things up in all kinds of ways. And so Jesus is here for US—he's not afraid of our mess. On the other hand, this is difficult news because it means God doesn't support our charade. He doesn't want us living as if the "highlights reel" of social media is the reality of life. He wants us to be real, and that takes more courage than being fake.

Ultimately, Jesus is asking us to keep our focus on our inside more than our outside. So how are you "cleaning the inside" of your cup these days? What do you do on an ongoing basis to connect with God, let go of bitterness, and receive grace? Are you spending as much time on your inside as you are on your outside?

Practice Take some time to journal in response to these questions: 1) Where am I most tempted to present my fake self instead of my real self? and 2) Where could my insides use some "cleaning" today? How can I go about that?

Devotion 18

*Truly my soul finds rest in God;/ my salvation comes
from him./ Truly he is my rock and my salvation;/
he is my fortress, I will never be shaken.*

PSALM 62:1–2

Unpredictability causes stress, and sometimes even anxiety and
fear. We like to know what to expect, but things in life are always
changing. Every time you walk through your front door, there is
something different, from what you're wearing and how you're
feeling to what's going on in your body. Every time you wake up
in the morning, it's a different moment and a different day.

So this metaphor that God gives of being a "rock" or a "fortress" is powerful. As everything else is in constant flux through
the course of each day, God is an anchor that keeps you moored.

During meditation practice, we find an "anchor" for our
attention—connecting our awareness to one particular thing as we
sit in silence. This might be God's presence, or it might be another
gift of God in the moment, such as your breath, a physical sensation, or sounds. Whatever that anchor is for you, know that God is
the ultimate rock in your life, your unshakeable fortress.

Practice Following the centering prayer guide on page
184–185, allow your awareness to rest on God's presence
as your rock, your anchor. While everything else might be
moving, you can know that God is solid. When you are finished, write a simple prayer of response in your journal.

Devotion 19

. . . we take captive every thought to make it obedient to Christ.

2 Corinthians 10:5

The mind is not always a safe place. Thoughts can be bullies, pushing us around and tearing us down. Negative thoughts create a lot of internal pain and can be destructive to your relationship with yourself, others, and God.

Fortunately, many of the thoughts we have simply are not true. God says that you can practice controlling your thought life so that it has less control over you, as you seek to be obedient to Christ who loves you and has your good at heart. Mindfulness helps with this, as you practice noticing thoughts as "passing experiences" that do not have to be believed, obeyed, or fed.

Catching thoughts early helps be intentional about your thought life. It's easier to redirect an untrue thought when it's a newborn monster rather than waiting until it's a full-grown Godzilla. But whatever size that thought has become by the time you notice it, Christian mindfulness teaches that you don't need to fear thoughts. God can quiet and redirect even the scariest thought monsters.

Practice We all have favorite thought monsters, recurring ones that show up when we're stressed or angry or sad. Take some time to jot down your most recurrent negative thoughts in your journal. This will increase your ability to notice them early next time they come around. God isn't scared of those thoughts and is ready to bring relief.

Devotion 20

Can any one of you by worrying add a single hour to your life [or single cubit to your height]?

MATTHEW 6:27

Dialectical Behavior Therapy teaches people to notice which behaviors are "effective" in reaching their goals. For example, if your goal in a class is an A, is it effective to scream at your teacher about the C that you received? Or might it be more effective to set up a meeting to explore study strategies for reaching your goal?

This is the point Jesus is making in this verse. Is your worrying really "effective?" Can you add anything to your life by worrying about it, or might there be a better way of reaching your goals?

We apply this principle in mindful yoga, where paying attention to tension helps us notice whether it is helpful. (Tension in your forehead won't help you hold a pose with your legs, so perhaps there is an option to smile and let it go.)

If you feel worry today, pay attention to whether that tension is helping you reach your goals. Maybe it's possible to release your grip on that worry just a little, as Jesus encourages you to do. He's in control.

Practice Following the stretching/yoga guide on page 170–171, practice noticing where there is tension in your body as you move through the practice. See if it is an option to let it go, as you bring your awareness to the movement or pose you intend to be focusing on. When you are finished, jot down some observations in your journal.

Devotion 21

*When the Pharisees saw this, they asked his disciples,
"Why does your teacher eat with tax collectors and
sinners?" On hearing this, Jesus said, "It is not
the healthy who need a doctor, but the sick."*

MATTHEW 9:11–12

God is SO not afraid of emotions. As our Great Physician, God knows that he has what we need when we are hurting. God can also see the big picture, and knows that our suffering will pass.

Jesus demonstrated this in his daily connection with people who were sick in body or spirit. He chose to hang out with people who were having a hard time. He accepted whatever they were going through as part of the human experience, something to be expected, and he knew that it wasn't too much for him (or for them). He responded with compassion and acceptance, not rejection.

We are invited to approach our difficult emotions and experiences the same way. We can have compassion with ourselves, staying with our own difficult feelings in the same way that Jesus stayed with the sick and the suffering during his time on earth. It's okay to struggle, and God is with us, with compassion.

Practice Following the lovingkindness/blessing guide on page 172–173, choose where you would like to focus your attention. Practice an attitude of compassion, seeing if you can stay with any difficult emotions you feel rather than rejecting them or judging them. When you are finished, jot down some observations in your journal.

Devotion 22

There is a way that appears to be right,
but in the end it leads to death.

PROVERBS 14:12

There are so many things we do without thinking, as if on auto-pilot. Sometimes, this is fine. Tying your shoes or driving a car are best done after lots of practice makes them automatic rather than thinking about each step every time.

But auto-pilot can get us in trouble when we have practiced things incorrectly. Many of our automatic thoughts fall in this category. Perhaps we have thought things so many times that they seem right when in fact, they are damaging. As the author of Proverbs says, some things that seem right are actually "the way to death."

Which of your thoughts seem right in the moment but are ultimately harmful? Some common examples might be "No one cares" or "I fail at everything I do." These thoughts are mental habits that do not bring life, growth, or joy. They are not from God.

Mindfulness practice puts a spotlight on your auto-pilot thoughts. If certain thoughts seem right but then "lead to death," it might be time to try some different thoughts! Even if the harmful thoughts still pop up, you don't have to follow them.

Practice Following the sitting practice guide on page 167, notice what auto-pilot thoughts come up for you. Are they life-giving or harmful? No need to change thoughts—just be curious about what "seems right," even when it's not. When you are finished, jot down some observations in your journal.

Devotion 23

. . . he went home to his upstairs room where the windows opened toward Jerusalem. Three times a day he got down on his knees and prayed, giving thanks to his God, just as he had done before.

DANIEL 6:10

Our routines have a huge impact on our overall wellbeing. This is true all the time, but especially during difficult times.

Daniel lived in captivity, oppressed by a government that had conquered and kidnapped his people. Praying three times a day was an established routine that kept him grounded in God through the traumas that he was enduring.

When a document was signed mandating that no one pray to anyone besides the king of Babylon, Daniel knew what was important—maintaining his routine of praying to God. He chose not to change that routine because he knew how important it was to him, his people, and God. If you know the rest of the story, you've heard that this routine led him to the lions' den, and ultimately out of the lions' den to proclaim God's deliverance.

What routines do you have each day? How are they impacting you, your people, and God? Are your routines ready to sustain you during times of trouble?

Practice Take a day to observe your routines. Notice what patterns you have related to sleeping, eating, socializing, social media, talking with God, working/studying, etc. Notice which of these routines are lifegiving for you and which bring you down. Take some time to write your observations in your journal.

Devotion 24

"Which of these three do you think was a neighbor to the man who fell into the hands of robbers?" The expert in the law replied, "The one who had mercy on him." Jesus told him, "Go and do likewise."

LUKE 10:36–37

Jesus tells this "good Samaritan" story to illustrate our tendency to dismiss and ignore suffering rather than show mercy. In his story, a man was attacked by robbers and left "half dead" on the side of the road. Two people came upon him as they are walking down the road, both of whom "passed by on the other side."

We've all done this—looked away when someone needed help. But we do this with ourselves too. We ignore our own suffering, giving our own feelings the silent treatment because we are afraid of them or don't know what to do with them.

The third person in Jesus' story "saw" and "took care." We can learn to see suffering and then show care, to be present to ourselves and others in the midst of difficulty with an attitude of mercy.

Practice Following the working with difficulty meditation guide on page 178–179, practice "seeing" any difficulty you are personally experiencing and showing mercy. You don't have to fix your difficulty, simply practice an attitude of compassion toward yourself. God will take care of the rest. When you are finished, jot down some observations in your journal.

Devotion 25

Taste and see that the Lord is good;
blessed is the one who takes refuge in him.

PSALM 34:8

We can think about God's goodness and sometimes feel happy emotions about it, but did you know we can also access it quite directly through our sense of taste? When the Psalmist encourages you to "taste . . . that the Lord is good," you might imagine biting into your favorite food, something that you love to taste. Whether that's a cookie or an apple or a piece of sushi, the pleasure you experience through your sense of taste is the goodness of God.

There are also tastes we don't enjoy that are good in different ways. Maybe you don't like the taste of raw broccoli or almonds or cabbage salad, but these foods provide nutrients and vitamins that humans need to live. Tastes that are unpleasant can still convey God's goodness by strengthening our bodies and minds.

God made your sense of taste to help you eat good food—food that brings you pleasure and nourishes your body. Like all of your senses, taste is a good gift from the God who loves you. God's good gifts remind us how good he is. "Taste . . . that the Lord is good."

Practice Following the sensing guide on page 180–181, choose a drink or small food item to use in exploring your sense of taste. Notice God's goodness in the taste of the food. When you are finished, jot down some observations in your journal.

Devotion 26

Yet this I call to mind/ and therefore I have hope:/ Because of the LORD's great love we are not consumed,/ for his compassions never fail./ They are new every morning;/ great is your faithfulness.

LAMENTATIONS 3:21–23

There is a redundancy to God's creation. Every morning, the sun comes up. Every season, the weather turns. Things start over again and again. Here's another morning. And then another one.

Somehow, each of these mornings is new. And Scripture tells us that each morning comes with new compassion from God. EVERY SINGLE DAY. New love, new compassion.

This reminds us that our life is full of new beginnings. Every single day. And our life is full of new compassion, every single day.

In mindfulness practice, we refer to this as "beginning again"—learning to see each moment and each day as a new beginning. You might be tempted to see your past failures or difficulties as defining who you are. But God never defines us by our past. God is in the business of new beginnings so that we get connected with new compassion every morning, and because of this we have hope. "Great is your faithfulness!"

Practice Following a mountain meditation on page 174–175, notice the newness of each morning that dawns on this image of yourself as a mountain. You are stable and strong, and you are also given new beginnings each and every day (every moment) from the God who loves you. When you are finished, jot down some observations in your journal.

Devotion 27

*. . . That is how it continued to be; the cloud covered it,
and at night it looked like fire. Whenever the cloud lifted
from above the tent, the Israelites set out; wherever
the cloud settled, the Israelites encamped.*

NUMBERS 9:15–17

Relationships with visible people can be hard enough, but having a relationship with an invisible God can feel especially challenging. You might forget more easily about a being that you can't see with your eyes, and even when you remember that God is there, you might find it difficult to know how to connect.

The Israelites were given a visible sign of God's presence as they journeyed through the wilderness—a fiery cloud. This God-cloud led them, telling them when to move and when to stay where they were. A pretty handy sign of God's presence, and one that you would think would be hard to ignore. But the reality is that the Israelites still struggled to see and follow God. Their story of journeying through the wilderness is not exactly one of communing with God at every step.

Whether your experiences of God are physical (senses), emotional (feelings), or cognitive (thoughts), chances are that you'll have to be intentional about experiencing God. It will take some work to notice God's presence and then pay attention. The intentionality is well worth it, so don't be afraid to do the work.

Practice Following a centering prayer guide on page 184–185, take some time to place your attention on God's presence. Acknowledge that God is with you. When you are finished, jot down some observations in your journal.

Devotion 28

"I am with you and will watch over you wherever you go, and I will bring you back to this land. I will not leave you until I have done what I have promised you."

GENESIS 28:15

Mindfulness practice brings our attention back to the present moment, over and over. This is different than our mind's natural tendency to wander into predictions about the future or rehashing of the past. When you practice mindfulness, you notice your mind wandering forward and backward, but you gently return your attention to what is happening right now.

Christians can practice mindfulness with an assurance that God holds the big picture. God promises good things for us, even when there are difficulties along the way. You can practice being present in the moment because God is actively fulfilling his promises for your future. Walking with you "wherever you go," never leaving you, always bringing you back to good things, over and over.

Being present in the moment allows you to notice the goodness that God is providing even in the midst of difficulties. As God fulfills his good promises, you will be more likely to notice at the time because you'll be practiced at staying present.

 Practice Following a breathing space guide on page 176–177, take a few minutes to rest your attention in the present moment. Whether you feel difficult or pleasant things here, he has good things in store and will never leave you. When you are finished, jot down some observations in your journal.

Devotion 29

Even my close friend,/ someone I trusted,/ one who shared my bread,/ has turned against me.

PSALM 41:9

All people need connection and belonging. This is why rejection can be so deeply wounding, whether actual or perceived. A romantic breakup, the loss of a friendship, or parental abandonment can all become lodged in our hearts and minds like splinters. Even daily miscommunications and conflicts are a challenge—no one gets along all the time since none of us are the same.

Most Bible stories include betrayal, rejection, miscommunication, and marginalization. The most prominent example is Jesus. When he was betrayed by Judas, one of his close followers, he used the words from this psalm to describe the experience: "He who shared my bread has turned against me" (John 13:18). He knew it was a fulfillment of prophesy, but it still felt personal.

God doesn't promise to take away our relational conflicts, but there is comfort knowing he understands. He's been there too.

Practice Bring to mind a mild communication difficulty. Take some time to briefly answer the following questions in your journal. 1) Describe the difficult communication and how it came about. 2) What did you want from the person and what did you actually get? 3) What did the person want from you and what did they actually get? 4) What did you feel during and after? 5) Is the difficulty resolved now? If not, what is your next step?

Devotion 30

For we are God's handiwork, created in Christ Jesus to do
good works, which God prepared in advance for us to do.

EPHESIANS 2:10

God made you for a purpose. You don't have to know what that's all about, but you do have an opportunity to observe yourself now as God's "handiwork." Like the handiwork of an architect or a watchmaker, the way you've been created is very intentional and specific.

One cool thing about how you've been created is your brain's fight-flight-freeze response, an internal alarm system to help protect you. When you feel threatened physically or psychologically, your body will automatically react to keep you safe before you even think about it. This might include your heartrate increasing, muscles tensing, and breath shortening, along with upset stomach, dilated pupils, and sweatiness. This is what stress and anxiety is about—the fight-flight-freeze system getting activated as your body attempts to protect you from perceived danger.

The fight-flight-freeze response can be scary if we think something is wrong. But that instinctual alarm system is natural and God-given, part of God's "handiwork" that is you.

Practice Write observations in your journal about how you show stress in your body (ex. tense shoulders), thoughts (ex. "I can't do this"), emotions (ex. anger), and behaviors/urges (ex. canceling plans). Know this type of response is natural and turns off eventually. It's part of God's handiwork!

Devotion 31

Then they sat on the ground with him for seven days and seven nights. No one said a word to him, because they saw how great his suffering was.

JOB 2:13

Job is famous for having some clueless friends who tried to blame his suffering on him. They talked for so long about Job's suffering being his own fault that it fills up 34 chapters of Scripture!

But before they launched into their long tirade, they actually started in exactly the right place. They sat on the ground in solidarity with Job, without speaking, simply being present.

Jesus took the same approach with Mary and Martha as they grieved the loss of their brother Lazarus. Even though Jesus knew that he would soon be raising Lazarus from the dead, he joined with his friends' suffering and wept, fully present with them.

Like Job's friends, we sometimes think we're supposed to have explanations and fixes for our friends' suffering. We're not. The most helpful thing to do when a friend is hurting is to be present. There may be times to offer words of wisdom or enjoyable diversions, but the most important thing you will ever do for your friend is to listen and grieve with them, just like Jesus showed us.

Practice Following the working with difficulty meditation guide on page 178–179, practice staying present to something that is difficult. This will help you be better prepared to stay present for friends during times of difficulty. When you are finished, jot down observations in your journal.

Devotion 32

*Have mercy on me, O God,/ according to
your unfailing love;/ according to your great
compassion/ blot out my transgressions.*

PSALM 51:1

What do you feel when you read this verse? What words jump out at you? Depending on what religious messages have been prevalent in your experience, you may hear the "mercy" part most loudly or you may hear the "my transgressions" part as dominant. If the "transgressions" part is louder, you might have the feeling that mercy is pretty far away.

Sometimes we forget that the whole point of the gospel of Jesus Christ is that our sins are forgiven. God has unfailing love and great compassion for us, and this was demonstrated in Jesus' death on the cross as atonement for our "transgressions." Our sins have been blotted out! This means that when we acknowledge our sin and pray "Have mercy on me, O God," we are simply receiving something that is already offered. We are already swimming in God's love and compassion.

God loves you. Your sins are forgiven. Receive his mercy, and rest in his compassion. There's nothing else you have to do.

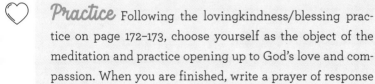 *Practice* Following the lovingkindness/blessing practice on page 172–173, choose yourself as the object of the meditation and practice opening up to God's love and compassion. When you are finished, write a prayer of response in your journal.

Devotion 33

. . . for it is God who works in you to will and to
act in order to fulfill his good purpose.

PHILIPPIANS 2:13

You're a work in progress. You're not a finished piece sitting on a museum shelf for others to view. You're not all polished, you're not stagnant. You're a living, breathing, developing, growing, learning human being. You're not supposed to be finished yet.

Think for a minute about how long you've been alive. How does this compare to the number of years that the universe has been in existence? It's a drop in the bucket. No matter how many years you live, it will be a drop in the bucket compared to the history of the universe.

So go easy on yourself. Expect to mess things up and get things wrong, to fail, to make mistakes. You'll be in lots of situations throughout your life where you're still trying to figure it out.

God is at work in you, so you can let go of the pressure to get it all right. No matter how many years you live, he will be shaping and molding you until the very end. And he will be doing that with the whole arc of the universe in mind, focused on fulfilling his good purpose in the big picture. How cool is that?

 Practice Following the mountain meditation guide on page 174–175, notice how a mountain is constantly changing and growing. Even as you are stable and rooted, you are constantly being formed and re-formed. When you are finished, jot down some observations in your journal.

Devotion 34

Carry each other's burdens, and in this way
you will fulfill the law of Christ.

GALATIANS 6:2

If someone has a heavy box, we might be able to literally carry that burden for a while until our arms get too tired. But what if their burden is depression, a terminal illness, or getting ghosted? There's not much we can do to change the difficult circumstances of other people, and it can be hard to know how to help.

There are times when our burden-carrying can be practical, like writing a card or helping with a difficult task, but praying for one another is one of the most important ways we can help. This doesn't have to be super formal. Whenever someone comes to mind in the midst of a day, you can imagine them in God's presence and ask God to be with them. As the Quakers say, you can "hold them up in the light" of Christ and then trust that God will do the rest. God loves that person even more than you and is providing everything they need.

You never need to fix things for other people, nor can you. But you can always hold them up in God's light as they are brought to your mind. God will do the rest.

Practice Following the lovingkindness/blessing guide on page 172–173, focus your attention on someone you know who is having a difficult time. As you extend compassionate blessing to them, recognize that your prayer is one way of carrying their burdens. God will do the rest.

Devotion 35

Then you will call, and the LORD will answer;
you will cry for help, and he will say: Here am I.

ISAIAH 58:9

Professionals in the mental health field know that the most powerful healing tool we have is to listen and be present for others. When people come to counseling in deep pain, there are plenty of techniques that counselors use to help, but there is nothing more powerful than listening well.

This is what God does with us. We call and he answers. We cry for help and he says, "Here am I." Whether or not we perceive God with us, God is with us.

Mindfulness is about learning to notice, and one of the things we can notice is that God is with us and that God's presence with us is healing. As strange as it sounds, we can also learn to be with ourselves, to mimic God as we say, "Here am I." Just like a counselor might listen well, stay with you in your pain, and show an attitude of understanding and compassion, you can do the same thing with yourself as a way to receive God's healing in the moment.

Practice Following the working with difficulty guide on page 178–179, notice the opportunity to be with yourself using an attitude of compassion, just as you imagine a counselor sitting with you in kindness and understanding. This is how God is with you—all the time, with compassion. When you are finished, jot down some observations in your journal.

Devotion 36

*May God be gracious to us and bless us/ and make his
face shine on us—/ so that your ways may be known
on earth,/ your salvation among all nations.*

PSALM 67:1–2

Imagine that someone unexpectedly drops a box on your doorstep
filled with a million dollars in cash. If you ignore the box, kicking it
to the curb before walking in your front door, you will miss out on
that blessing. If you open up the box, you will most likely be filled
with excitement, wonder, and gratitude to the giver. You're likely
to tell lots of people about the cash and the surprise benefactor.

This is what God's blessings are like. We miss most of them,
ignoring them and kicking them to the curb. Mindfulness practice
can help us notice the blessings in each moment, which sets us up
to be grateful to God and tell others about him.

Fortunately, God is eager to bless us. He is gracious to us, and
he shines on us through each day. This doesn't mean we have to
feel happy all the time, but it can be helpful to take some time each
day to pay attention to what is in the moment so that we don't miss
too much of what God is showering upon us.

Practice Following the walking/wheeling meditation on
page 168–169, observe your ability to move through space
as one of God's everyday blessings—but it's actually quite
miraculous. Notice how God makes himself known through
this miracle of walking or wheeling! When you are finished,
jot down some observations in your journal.

Devotion 37

*I thank my God every time I remember you. In all my prayers
for all of you, I always pray with joy. . . . It is right for me to
feel this way about all of you, since I have you in my heart
and, whether I am in chains or defending and confirming
the gospel, all of you share in God's grace with me.*

PHILIPPIANS 1:3–4, 7

The Apostle Paul faced intense rejection throughout his life, to
the point of being put in prison and brutally attacked on a regular basis. It makes sense that he needed to balance that out with
reminders that he belonged somewhere. He was intentional about
keeping those he loved in his heart, and he made a point of remem-
bering them with gratitude and joy on a regular basis.

It's worthwhile to identify people you care about and practice
holding them in your heart. Maybe it's a family member or friend, or
even a famous person that you've never met but brings you joy when
you think of them. Maybe it's a group that you belong to. Maybe
"your people" are changing, which is totally normal. But take some
time to think about the people you're connected to, noticing how
you share life together, and then keep them in your heart.

Practice Following the guide for lovingkindness/bless-
ing on page 172–173, identify a person you love or admire
and hold them as the object of your attention during the
practice. Hold them in your heart, nurturing any feelings of
warmth that might come up. When you are finished, write a
prayer of thanksgiving for the people you love.

Devotion 38

Be kind and compassionate to one another, forgiving each other, just as in Christ God forgave you.

EPHESIANS 4:32

People can be rough to put up with. Sometimes it seems like life would be a lot easier if everyone else would just be normal! So it's no small task to "be kind and compassionate to one another, forgiving each other."

The truth is that we are all difficult people, and we are all in need of compassion. While this might be a little hard to swallow (most of us aren't trying to be difficult!), it's actually great news. We can't be perfect, and that's okay because all is forgiven. God is kind and compassionate toward you. He loves you just as you are!

Practice being kind and compassionate to others in their difficulties. You won't always get it right—we all have grudges and self-righteous attitudes that are pretty hard to let go of! But God is your guide, teaching you, and we can all grow in our ability over time to let go of pettiness and treat each other with compassion.

Practice Following the lovingkindness/blessing meditation on page 172–173, focus your practice on someone who is difficult for you. This is not the time to choose the most difficult person in your life. But think of someone who has hurt your feelings or annoyed you in some way, and see if you can practice extending the same compassion to them that you have received from God. When you are finished, write a brief prayer of blessing for that person in your journal.

Devotion 39

We love because he first loved us.

1 JOHN 4:19

Love can look so starry-eyed and sweet in the movies, with so much of the complexity taken out. But God's love story with us is real life. It's messy and confusing and sometimes hard. Like any real-life love story, that's what makes it so beautiful—it's hard-won, tried in the fires of adversity.

When we read that God "first loved us," are we pausing to grasp what this means? God is the initiator in this love story. He has put up with rejection, insensitivity, and lots of cluelessness from us, and he has stayed persistent through it all. He has endured intense physical pain and immeasurable emotional agony on our behalf through his death on the cross, and he has stayed present even when we've completely ignored him. He has continued to send us messages of his love through creation, through people who love us, and through that still, small voice in our hearts that reminds us he is there. He does not give up on us.

This is the most beautiful love story of all time. Noticing the love of God is one of the ways we can wake up our hearts to love ourselves, to love others, and to love God back. Let's pay attention!

 Practice Following the breathing space practice on page 176–177, take some time to settle into this moment with an awareness of God's ever-present, never-giving-up, ever-initiating love for us. God is here. When you are finished, jot down some observations in your journal.

Devotion 40

*"As the Father has loved me, so have I
loved you. Now remain in my love."*

JOHN 15:9

Jesus knew he was loved by the Father, and he passed that love on to you. He invites you to remain in that love. But it's often easier to remain in self-criticism or self-contempt than in love.

One way to practice remaining in God's love is to develop a physical gesture of care toward yourself. Sometimes others show their love or affection for you by giving a hug, holding your hand, or smiling at you. You can learn to show yourself love and affection in similar ways. Some examples include a hand (or both hands) on your heart, wrapping your arms around yourself in a gentle hug, holding your own hand (by resting one hand in the palm of the other), or smiling. Trying to *think* your way into feeling loved is sometimes a challenge, and so showing yourself love with a physical gesture is another way to help God's love sink in more effectively.

It's kind of like the difference between someone saying "I love you" from a distance versus someone coming close, putting their hand on your shoulder, and looking at you with affection. That physical gesture makes a big difference in your ability to absorb the message.

Practice Take a couple minutes to experiment with different physical gestures that convey love toward yourself (using the examples above). Once you have found one that feels nice for you, practice sitting in that physical position for a minute and experiencing God's love.

Devotion 41

Shortly before dawn Jesus went out to them, walking on the lake. When the disciples saw him walking on the lake, they were terrified. "It's a ghost," they said, and cried out in fear. But Jesus immediately said to them: "Take courage! It is I. Don't be afraid."

MATTHEW 14:25–27

It's kind of funny that sometimes we not only fail to notice God's presence, but that when we do notice God we don't necessarily recognize him. We sometimes even get freaked out by him! God is different enough from us that we are often surprised at how he shows up.

In this story, Jesus' disciples cry out "It's a ghost" when they see him. They weren't expecting a person walking on the lake, so it caused alarm. Jesus had to actually say "It is I," as in "Chill out dudes, it's just me." This is what happens whenever an angel is sent by God as well. The angel has to say "Don't be afraid." The reality is that we don't always recognize God or his messengers, and we're not always very welcoming in our first response.

Life is a long practice in learning to notice God and then recognize him, whatever our initial emotion. When God shows up, it will often be in ways we don't expect. Be on the lookout!

Practice Following the guide for centering prayer on page 184–185, take some time to practice awareness of God. Whether or not you recognize it, and whatever your emotion is right now, God is present with you. Then write a prayer in your journal committing to recognize God as much as you can!

"I am making everything new!"
REVELATION 21:5

"There's nothing to do." "I'm so bored." "Why do I have to do this over again?" If you've ever said (or thought) something like this, you're not alone. Life can sometimes feel a bit dull or redundant.

In reality, every single moment we are alive is different from every other moment. You've never taken this breath before. You've never had this exact set of feelings, thoughts, physical sensations, and circumstances. When we talk about God as Creator, it's not just that he made the world a long time ago. It's that he's still creating in every single moment of our lives, making new stuff. Things are always changing!

The next time you're bored, consider taking a moment to actually pay attention to what is in the moment. Be curious about what it's like to be you right now—this breath, this body, this experience with God. The next moment will be different, and you want to be ready to experience the newness of God's work!

Practice Choose a routine hygiene activity that you typically do without paying much attention, such as brushing your teeth, washing your face, or shampooing your hair. Do that activity with your full attention on the experience, directly noticing what it is like for you as a "new" experience in this moment. When you are finished, jot down some observations in your journal.

Devotion 43

He tends his flock like a shepherd:/ He gathers the
lambs in his arms/ and carries them close to his
heart;/ he gently leads those that have young.

ISAIAH 40:11

Being in nature is one of the ways God often calms our souls, and he does this even through nature imagery used in Scripture. In this verse, God describes us as sheep carried close to his heart and led gently along.

Maybe God uses all this nature imagery because it helps us to know that we ourselves are part of nature. It's easy to think that our human stories really matter and it's all about how we impact the world. And while you do matter a great deal, your actual significance lies in being part of God's grand story that we all carry out together as his creation. We are loved by God, and that matters.

You are part of this amazing world God has created. When you see trees, plants, birds, animals, and all kinds of living beings, you can know that you belong to all of this. God cares for you as part of nature, like a sheep, and you are never alone in this big, beautiful world that he created.

Practice Take some time to observe nature in whatever way it is available to you (inside or outside). Notice whatever is coming through your senses as you observe the natural world (sounds, sight of shapes and colors, feelings on your skin, etc.), and thank God that you are a loved part of the natural world that he has created.

*For every house is built by someone, but
God is the builder of everything.*

HEBREWS 3:4

There's a pretty good chance you're living in a house built by someone besides you, and scores of other people helped create the materials for it. From designing to creating to transporting to installing . . . there are SO many folks who have worked to prepare your home for you. Same with the chair you're sitting in or the floor you're standing on. It's pretty remarkable how dependent we are on people we don't even know to build these things.

And beyond all of those human creators and builders (and cleaners and repairers), there is God who is "the builder of everything." You are literally occupying physical spaces that God has prepared for you, even when you're at school or church or the grocery store. These buildings are signs of God's care for you.

There may be some big ways you are waiting for God to show up with an answered prayer or a changed circumstance. Keep talking to God about those, but don't forget to notice the spaces that he's built for you already. "God is the builder of everything."

Practice Take a moment to notice the house or building that you are in. Notice that many people have been involved in creating the building and all the things in it. Allow yourself a couple minutes for that to sink in—you are receiving a gift of shelter in this moment, provided by so many people, and "God is the builder of everything." You are blessed.

Devotion 45

. . . He has sent me to bind up the brokenhearted . . .

ISAIAH 61:1

Maybe you've gone through a breakup or rejection, or maybe you've had a parent or trusted person let you down in a big way. Heartbreak is painful, sometimes even physically, and it can take a long time to heal.

God's response to our broken-heartedness is to bind us up like a parent who puts a bandage on a wounded knee or a doctor who puts a cast on a fractured arm. Scripture also says God "saves those who are crushed in spirit" (Psalm 34:18). When we're broken or crushed, he doesn't condemn us or push us along, but instead takes care of us until we recover from our wounds and feel better.

When you are brokenhearted, how likely are you to show yourself care? Do you "bind up" your heart, or do you beat up on yourself? Do you show yourself compassion and kindness, or do you use a harsh tone with yourself when you're hurting?

God has nothing but compassion for you when you are brokenhearted. You might try showing yourself some love today as well.

Practice Following the body scan guide on page 166, notice how God is caring for all of your body, mind, and spirit in this moment, especially any parts that are hurting or feel "broken" (both physical and emotional). See if you can show yourself some kindness, knowing that God is close to those who are brokenhearted. When you are finished, jot down some observations in your journal.

Devotion 46

*When Jesus spoke again to the people, he said, "I am
the light of the world. Whoever follows me will never
walk in darkness, but will have the light of life."*

JOHN 8:12

Karl Marx famously described religion as "the opium of the
people," as if faith numbs us while making us unaware in the
process (like drugs). Maybe we sometimes would like religion to
numb our suffering, but Jesus described himself as "light." This
implies that Christian faith helps you be *more* aware. And far from
being drug-like, it sharpens your understanding of reality.

With Jesus, we can see more! Sometimes this is challenging—
we're more likely to notice things like people's suffering and the sin
in our own lives. But living in Jesus' light brings a more vital life. It
makes us more likely to notice the healing power of prayer, the bound-
less provision of God, and the immeasurable beauty of forgiveness.

Being present to our lives means we feel it all, not just the stuff
we like, but it also means we are fully alive! Living in Jesus' light
lets us take in all the goodness. Sign me up for that!

Practice Take a moment to "see" the moment you are in
right now. You can keep your eyes open or closed, but just
notice how things are for you right now—thoughts, feelings,
physical sensations, etc. Allow yourself in this moment to be
more aware of your present moment experience, knowing
that you are sitting in God's illuminating presence. When
you are finished, jot down some observations in your journal.

Devotion 47

But we have this treasure in jars of clay to show that this all-surpassing power is from God and not from us.

2 CORINTHIANS 4:7

God is super powerful, and we are not. We're more like fragile clay jars. But God lives inside of us! There's a delicate balance in our self-esteem here—we know we have lots of power (it shines out every day!), but we also know that we're super fragile.

These are both true. We stay humble because of the "jars of clay" part. We stay awed by ourselves and one another because of God's "all-surpassing power" housed in us. We get to be a team with God, so close that he lives inside us all the time, all mixed up together as one unit. Our fragility does not take away from God's power that lives within us.

When you pay attention through mindfulness practice, you'll notice parts of yourself that feel weak and others that feel strong. This reflects the reality of you as a clay jar housing "all-surpassing power." So while you're acknowledging your fragility, see if you can also acknowledge God's power in you.

Practice Notice yourself where you are right now. Whether you're most aware of your weakness or strength in this moment, give yourself (and God within you) a smile—lift the corners of your mouth slightly, allow your eyes to smile, relax your shoulders. Notice that God has chosen to house his power in your jar of clay, then carry on with your day.

Devotion 48

For I desire mercy, not sacrifice,
and acknowledgment of God rather than burnt offerings.

HOSEA 6:6

Legalism is the belief that we are saved by excessive conformity to rules, laws, and moral codes. While this might sound like something that's just for the Pharisees or other "super religious" people, we're all at risk of trying to earn our goodness by doing the right stuff, and this is true even for those who do not follow Christ.

There were a lot of rules back in Old Testament times, but even then, God said this remarkable thing: "I desire mercy, not sacrifice." God is looking for our hearts to be turned toward him with acknowledgment instead of getting all wrapped up in legalism, thinking that we need to earn our salvation by being perfect. He is looking for us to be less about sacrifices and more about mercy and acknowledgment of him.

Mindfulness practice can help you notice any patterns of legalism in your own thinking. It can help you release unnecessary pressure to earn salvation through perfectionism, inviting you into the ease of simply being with God and acknowledging his mercy. God does not desire perfection or legalism. He offers mercy instead.

 Practice Following the breathing space guide on page 176–177, notice any areas of tension in your body or mind. Notice the option to release some of that tension as you soften your shoulders, your eyes, and your heart. When you are finished, jot down some observations in your journal.

Devotion 49

My times are in your hands.

PSALM 31:15

With the amount of time we spend rehashing the past, it can seem surprising that we can't change it—it's already done. Also, the future is not happening yet, so we have no control over that either. The only place that we have any control is the present, and even there our control is more limited than we would like.

Fortunately, your past, present, and future—all of your times—are in God's hands. It's okay that your control is minimal because God's control is maximal. He doesn't make things nice-feeling all the time, but he is always working for your long-term good.

Focusing on the past or the future is an attempt to control parts of our story that we cannot. You can rest in the knowledge that God has all of your times in his hands. What is here is already here. Focusing on the present allows you to be awake for what God is up to in this moment, and it is the best use of your energy.

Practice Following the walking/wheeling guide on page 168–169, notice the tendency of your mind to move out of the present moment into stories about the past and future as you move. Focusing on your physical sensations of movement can help you anchor in the present because your body can't travel into the past or future—it's always in the here-and-now. As you move physically through space and time, notice that all of your times are in God's hands.

Devotion 50

Surely your goodness and love will follow me/ all the days of my life,/ and I will dwell in the house of the LORD/ forever.

PSALM 23:6

Can you think of a place that feels like home to you? It might be your actual house, or it might be a different place that is familiar and welcoming. (As they say, "home is where the heart is!")

When you center your life on God, it's like you are making your home with him. The psalmist describes this as to "dwell in the house of the Lord," a house where goodness and love abound. God offers goodness and love as our life's center, our home.

Having no home can be distressing. You may have experienced this literally, or maybe more figuratively and emotionally. Or maybe you've always had a strong sense of home. The cool thing is that whatever your earthly experience of home, you always have a home with God and it's always a good place to be.

Practicing mindfulness is one way to cultivate a feeling of being at home with yourself, and this can help you further ground your sense of home in God. As you learn to feel at home in your own body, mind, and spirit, know that you also dwell with God. God follows you every day with goodness and love, and sharing a home with him is the best place to be.

Practice Following the body scan guide on page 166, practice the experience of yourself as home—a home that you share with your creator God. When you are finished, jot down some observations in your journal.

Devotion 51

*For you created my inmost being;/ you knit me
together in my mother's womb./ I praise you
because I am fearfully and wonderfully made;/ your
works are wonderful,/ I know that full well.*

PSALM 139:13–14

The human body is a wonderful creation. Even after centuries of study and continuous advances in medical technology, we can still barely understand how it all works.

It's kind of fun to imagine God knitting this together, your body. Laying muscles over bones, arranging the brain's communication systems, putting in the tubing of arteries and veins to carry blood, crafting the shape of your face and limbs then stepping back and saying "It is good" as he did with all of his creation.

And whatever kind of relationship you have with your biological mother now, God used her womb back in the day as a studio for making you—a workbench upon which to knit you together. Pretty wild!

There's much we will never understand about the human body, but those of us who pay attention will always find glimpses of our Creator in these bodies we have been given. We have truly been wonderfully made. We are wonderful works of God.

Practice Following the body scan guide on page 166, spend some time paying attention to this wonderful creation of God—your body! When you are finished, jot down some observations in your journal.

Devotion 52

Know that the L<small>ORD</small> is God. / It is he who made us, and we are his; / we are his people, the sheep of his pasture.

PSALM 100:3

There will be times you feel lonely, maybe intensely. In reality, you are part of a flock cared for by God, who watches over you as a shepherd with sheep. We are all the "sheep of his pasture."

You cannot shepherd yourself, and you cannot get all of your needs met on your own. You do not have to understand everything, and you are not responsible for the rest of the flock either. While that can be a little scary, it can also be comforting to let yourself be a sheep. You're not in charge here—you're part of the flock, tended by God.

Let yourself be like a sheep today. Notice what's provided for you by God (maybe food, water, shelter, other sheep in the flock). Stay close to God, your good shepherd, and don't lose sight of those other sheep too. You belong to God, just like sheep belong to a shepherd, and we're all in this together.

Practice Take a moment to notice yourself where you are, then become aware of other people in your environment. You might start with a small circle around you, and then slowly enlarge that circle to take in more and more people, until you've eventually gone from awareness of yourself to awareness of all the people in a very large vicinity, (even the whole world). You and all of these people are together in God's flock, made and tended by him.

Devotion 53

Though the fig tree does not bud/ and there are no grapes on the vines,/ though the olive crop fails/ and the fields produce no food,/ though there are no sheep in the pen/ and no cattle in the stalls,/ yet I will rejoice in the LORD,/ I will be joyful in God my Savior./ The Sovereign LORD is my strength;/ he makes my feet like the feet of a deer,/ he enables me to tread on the heights.

HABAKKUK 3:17–19

Nature has a cycle to it. No flower blooms all the time, no animal lives forever. Sometimes there are seasons when crops fail.

These cycles remind us that our wellbeing depends on God. We cannot have what we need without God's provision. This gives us the freedom to rejoice in any circumstance, knowing that our strength comes from God, not ourselves.

This doesn't mean we have to be happy and strong all the time. But psychological research supports the truth that most of our happiness does not depend on our circumstance. Our engagement in habits of wellness such as prayer, meditation, exercise, social connection, and journaling is a much better predictor of happiness. In order to access God's strength in hard seasons, we have to dig from a deeper well than our momentary circumstances and look to the God who cares for us through all of the cycles of life.

Practice Following the stretching/yoga guide on page 170–171, use this practice to get in touch with your body. As you move, allow your body to experience the strength of the Lord, no matter what season you are in. When you are finished, jot down some observations in your journal.

Devotion 54

I remain confident of this:/ I will see the goodness of the LORD/ in the land of the living./ Wait for the LORD;/ be strong and take heart/ and wait for the LORD.

PSALM 27:13–14

There is goodness present in each moment. That doesn't mean we see it though. Sometimes our hurt gets in the way, and lots of times we're just not paying attention.

The best way to see the goodness in a moment is to wait with careful attention. Don't just wait for changed circumstances in the future, though. Instead, wait with anticipation of what you might notice in the present moment. What goodness will emerge in your consciousness as you pay attention?

Mindfulness practices are a good way to do this—they help us learn to pay attention and to see what is good in the moment. Even when we notice things that are difficult, we can let go of our resistance to those difficulties and wait with open attention to see what goodness might emerge. "Take heart and wait for the Lord." He is always giving you something good, right here in the moment.

Practice Sit still for about two minutes, beginning with a deep breath and then moving your attention from your thoughts into your body with a direct awareness of your physical sensations. Then wait and see what "goodness" might emerge as you pay attention. When you are finished, jot a couple notes in your journal about the good thing(s) you noticed in the moment.

Devotion 55

"Therefore I tell you, do not worry about your life, what you will eat or drink; or about your body, what you will wear. ... Look at the birds of the air; they do not sow or reap or store away in barns, and yet your heavenly Father feeds them. Are you not much more valuable than they?"

MATTHEW 6:25–26

When someone who loves you sees you stressed out, they might give you a hug and then say with a wink "Don't worry, God's got your back." This is kind of what Jesus is doing in this verse. With a wink and a little joke about the birds, he's saying "Relax—aren't you worth more than the birds?" He's not saying don't feel anxious, but he's encouraging you to smile at your worried thoughts and practice letting go so you can notice God's provision showing up.

Jesus is also pointing out how creation is full of reminders of God providing. We don't need to stay wrapped up in worried thoughts. We don't need to obsessively hold on to things in fear of not having enough. Birds simply follow their God-given instincts, and God provides.

As much as you can, keep life simple, like the birds. Let go the worry and the stress. God will give you what you need.

 Practice Following the sitting practice guide on page 167, practice noticing your own worried thoughts with the same wink and sense of humor that Jesus has for your worries. "Aren't you worth more than the birds?" When you are finished, jot down some observations in your journal.

Devotion 56

For you have been born again, not of perishable seed, but of imperishable, through the living and enduring word of God.

1 PETER 1:23

The farther we get in life, the more stories we develop about ourselves and the more expectations we have of how life will go. But these stories are not facts—they're more like thinking shortcuts we've developed that are not always true. These shortcuts can limit our ability to clearly see the full picture of ourselves and others, and they trick us into thinking we can't change.

In what ways do you tend to think "I'm always like this" or "People always do that?" These thoughts can make you lose sight of how you and others are. You'll get more accurate information by avoiding the shortcuts in order to notice how things actually are now.

You are offered new beginnings all the time—but you have to notice how things are "right in this moment" so you can see those opportunities for rebirth. As we are reborn, God reminds us that our changes come from seed that is "imperishable" and "enduring." In other words, God is a constant for you through all of your new beginnings.

Practice Following the walking/wheeling meditation guide on page 168–169, practice noticing how each step or movement is a new beginning. God is in the business of re-birth, and you can experience "beginning again" with each step you take or each movement. When you are finished, jot down some observations in your journal.

Devotion 57

People were also bringing babies to Jesus for him to place his hands on them. When the disciples saw this, they rebuked them. But Jesus called the children to him and said, "Let the little children come to me, and do not hinder them, for the kingdom of God belongs to such as these. Truly I tell you, anyone who will not receive the kingdom of God like a little child will never enter it."

LUKE 18:15–17

Little kids don't know very much yet and it turns out that not knowing very much is a great way to come to Jesus. That way we're more ready to learn and more open to what God wants to show us.

In this Bible story, Jesus encourages all of us to be more like the children he was putting his arms around and blessing, which is something we could all use at any age. We don't have to understand a bunch of fancy stuff in order to be loved and blessed by God.

Instead of "not knowing," we often want to approach life as experts that have it figured out. But this can actually close us off from our blessing and keep us from learning new stuff. When we open our minds like little children, the world is full of surprise and growth. So be open, ready to learn, and expect to be delightfully surprised with blessings from Jesus along the way!

Practice Following the eating meditation guide on page 182–183, take time to experience your food. Practice the "not knowing" attitude of a child as you eat, being curious about what you might experience if this was your first time. When you are finished, jot down some observations in your journal.

Devotion 58

"Look," [Stephen] said, "I see heaven open and the Son of Man standing at the right hand of God." At this they covered their ears and, yelling at the top of their voices, they all rushed at him, dragged him out of the city and began to stone him.

ACTS 7:56–58

Stephen was on trial for his religious beliefs when he started describing a vision of heaven. How cool is that, to have a glimpse into God's throne room? But rather than listening to him describe more, the people covered their ears.

Lots of us tend to do this. When we hear something we're uncomfortable with, we stop listening. Someone says something we disagree with, and we respond by tuning them out or attacking.

It's not just silly to stop listening, it can be deadly. In Stephen's case, this was literal. The people covered their ears and then stoned him to death. In most cases, the "death" that occurs when we stop listening is the end of a relationship, or our wellbeing.

Listening is especially important when we disagree with someone or when we feel afraid. When you feel the urge to cover your ears, see if you can instead turn toward people and hear what they have to say. Whether or not you end up agreeing, you might learn something new and see more of God in the process.

Practice Watch for an opportunity to listen deeply to someone that you disagree with. See if you can turn toward them and get curious about their perspective. Whether or not you change your mind, you might be surprised at what you learn.

Devotion 59

Surely he will save you from the fowler's snare
and from the deadly pestilence.
He will cover you with his feathers,
and under his wings you will find refuge;
his faithfulness will be your shield and rampart.

PSALM 91:3–4

Life is kind of like a good movie or novel—there is lots of difficulty and danger, and we're often in suspense to see how things are going to work out in the end. This can be the case whether the difficulty is a small friendship challenge or a major terminal illness.

In this image from the psalms, we see how God shelters us through life's dangers. He's like a winged bird protecting its babies. He's like a shield or castle wall protecting its inhabitants. Your life might be a little more of an action-packed story than you would like, but like any good story, you can know that it includes just enough protection and provision from God so that you make it through.

There will be danger and suspense along the way, but God wrote the whole story and he has your soul's good at heart. He is for you, covering you, shielding you, seeing you through.

Practice Following the working with difficulty meditation guide on page 178–179, practice noticing how God is with you in your difficulty. You might even want to imagine yourself under his wings. The battle may be fierce, but you are cared for by God, the author of your story. When you are finished, jot down some observations in your journal.

Devotion 60

Then the LORD spoke to Job out of the storm. He said:/ "Who is this that obscures my plans/ with words without knowledge?/ "Where were you when I laid the earth's foundation?/ Tell me, if you understand.

JOB 38:1–2, 4

God was intimately involved in the creation of the world, and continues to be intimately involved in every detail of creation—keeping the earth spinning at just the right rate, just the right distance from the sun. This level of understanding about the universe is far beyond human comprehension. Even with giant leaps in our scientific understanding, humans will never understand most of the basics about creation. As God pointed out to Job, we were not there when he laid the earth's foundation, and most of our supposed "knowledge" clouds up our vision of what God is up to.

This frees us up to stop trying so hard. We can still find joy and meaning in the quest for knowledge, and we can still progress in our understanding of the world, but we will feel freer when we remember that God will always be the only one who knows it all. Our understanding is like that of curious little children and God is like the parent who smiles at us fondly and sees the big picture.

Practice Following the guide for centering prayer on page 184–185, notice your mind's movement back to what you think you "know" and bring your attention back to God's presence in the moment. When you are finished, jot down some observations in your journal.

Devotion 61

"My grace is sufficient for you, for my power is made perfect in weakness."

2 CORINTHIANS 12:9

Sometimes we work too hard to get things right and to please people. Our hard work can really pay off (like when you study in preparation for a difficult test). But there are other times that our hard work keeps us in the false belief that we have to do everything by ourselves and get it all right all the time.

God is clear in Scripture that he is not dependent on human power or knowledge to accomplish his purposes. Verses like this suggest his power grows in the context of your weakness. So being a Christian is not about being strong and put-together. It's more about acknowledging your weakness so that you can accept God's grace and be a vessel for *his* power.

God has everything you need. You don't have to get it all right. You don't have to please everyone. God's grace is sufficient, making his power perfect in your weakness.

Practice Following the walking/wheeling guide on page 168–169, notice how your body works with weakness to accomplish movement through space. Perhaps there is wobbling or other adjustments involved in staying stable and straight. Your "weakness" is woven together with the "power" provided by God, the grace that sustains you. When you are finished, jot a couple notes in your journal about whatever you noticed during the practice.

Devotion 62

God is love. Whoever lives in love lives in God, and God in them. This is how love is made complete among us . . .

1 JOHN 4:16–17

You can't manufacture love on your own, and you can't force love in yourself or your community. You can, however, "live" in love as a way to receive what God has for you. Then love can also "live" in you.

You might live in a house, in a community, in a country. This refers to where your body lives and also where you experience connection and belonging. Same with living in God. Your body is with God all the time, and God also provides you with a place of connection and belonging (whether or not you notice).

Other translations of this verse refer to "abiding" instead of "living" in God. You might picture this as relaxing, chilling, or moving in with. We are learning to settle into love (which is God) like kittens curl up with their mother cat or little children pile up on a couch together to watch a good show. In this way, God's love lives in us and comes to completion among us.

Practice Following the body scan guide on page 166, notice how your body is "living" here in this moment which is where God is. You are living in God and his love, and tuning into your body can be a way to remember this. When you are finished, jot down some observations in your journal.

Devotion 63

Are not two sparrows sold for a penny? Yet not one of them will fall to the ground outside your Father's care.

MATTHEW 10:29

Sparrows may be common and cheap when sold at the market, but they have a Father who cares for them deeply. God is paying really careful attention to his creation, even down to the level of a small bird falling to the ground. In this verse, Jesus goes on to say that "even the very hairs of your head are all numbered. So don't be afraid; you are worth more than many sparrows" (Matthew 10:30–31).

There may be times when you feel overlooked and neglected, lonely and isolated. You might think no one cares or listens, or even that no one notices whether or not you are here. But these are all lies of Satan, who tries to convince us that we don't matter in the world. These lies create suffering in our lives. They make our minds feel like unsafe places.

The truth is that every sparrow, every hair, every detail of creation matters—and you are part of the creation. The world is carefully designed by God, and he made you (and each of us) to be a part of it. You are noticed, treasured, and cared for.

Practice Following the eating meditation guide on page 182–183, receive your food as a way God is noticing your needs right now and providing for you. He cares. When you are finished, write a simple prayer of response to God in your journal.

Devotion 64

We know that in all things God works for the good of those who love him, who have been called according to his purpose.

ROMANS 8:28

The story of the universe is long, as is the story of your life. You live one moment at a time, and you will only catch small glimpses of your story at a time, much less the story of the universe. In fact, only God ever knows the whole story.

It can be reassuring to remember that we just see a little part of the puzzle at a time. What seems huge now may seem small later. What seems small now may take on much greater significance for us later. Each moment, day, and event of our life is like one dot on a connect-the-dot—it may seem just like a tiny dot, but it's part of a whole picture that will eventually come into view.

When you're not sure of the way forward or things seem dark, rest assured that this moment is just one little dot in a very large picture. God sees the whole picture and holds the whole story of your life (and of the even bigger universe). He is working toward your good because he loves you, and the final picture is already beautiful.

 Practice Following the mountain meditation guide on page 174–175, notice how many small pieces of a mountain make up the mountain's big story. The changing weather patterns, animals, and geological shifts all contribute to the beauty of the landscape over time. When you are finished, jot some notes in your journal about what you noticed.

Devotion 65

Whoever loves money never has enough; whoever loves wealth is never satisfied with their income.

ECCLESIASTES 5:10

Research shows that once people's basic needs of food and shelter are met, more money does not increase happiness. And yet most of us keep fighting for a bigger piece of the pie. It really seems like more would make you happier.

It's possible (even common) for a person to live their whole life unsatisfied, always wishing they had something more. The root of this is a love of money. But more money does not bring happiness or satisfaction. You can learn to notice these unrealistic expectations about money and stuff bringing happiness. If you want to live with a feeling of satisfaction, knowing that you have enough, practice turning away from a love of money.

What brings happiness? Connecting with people, showing compassion (to yourself and others), engaging in meaningful pursuits, serving others, caring for your body, and prayer/meditation. These are consistent with Scripture and with psychological research. Happiness is available, but not through money.

Practice Following the sitting practice guide on page 167, notice what desires pop up in your thoughts and how your mind expects to gain happiness. Practice coming back to how things are in this moment, where you are provided for and have everything you need. When you are finished, jot down some observations in your journal.

Devotion 66

Cast all your anxiety on him because he cares for you.

1 PETER 5:7

To cast something is to throw it. Imagine casting your trash into a garbage can or clothes into a washing machine. There can be a relief in getting rid of something heavy, difficult, or unpleasant.

Anxiety often feels unpleasant, and God is eager for you to cast it on him because he cares for you. Anxiety can seep into our thinking, our brain gripping onto it like a stone that we turn over, again and again. We review the same thoughts, make the same judgments, predict the same doom. Anxiety does not tend to lead us to new conclusions or solutions, it simply keeps us gripping the same thoughts.

God invites you to loosen your grip on any anxious thoughts you are carrying around. You can use a mindfulness practice to notice how you are holding onto the thoughts, and see if it's possible to step back, open up your hand, and cast that anxiety. You may find that there are some much more rewarding things for you to think about, once your mind is freed!

 Practice Following the stretching/yoga meditation on page 170–171, notice ways that your muscles are holding in anxious tension (such as in the shoulder or face area). Use the stretches to open up your body and mind to release that tension to God, casting your anxieties upon him because he cares for you. When you are finished, write a brief prayer of surrender in your journal.

The Lord said, "You have been concerned about this plant, though you did not tend it or make it grow. It sprang up overnight and died overnight."

JONAH 4:10

Plants grow without us. While we *can* tend them and set up the best conditions possible for growth, we cannot make them grow. Only God can do that. There are bajillions of plants that are not tended by humans. They spring up and die within God's care alone.

There are a lot of other things that happen without us having to do anything about them. Breathing is a good example—you don't have to create or force your breath to make it happen, you just receive it from God in each moment. In fact, you can't make yourself breathe, and there's not really any other part of living that we can force to happen without God's care. Only God creates and sustains life, even if we tinker with it along the way.

A lot of anxiety can come from trying to make things happen or to control things that are from God alone. Jonah was really worked up about a plant that sprang up and then died, even though that all happened outside of his control. Is there anything you're worked up about that is out of your control, that you could let go? God is sustaining you and all of the natural world. To receive it is enough.

Practice Following the breathing space guide on page 176–177, notice how you do not make yourself grow or breathe but God is sustaining you right now. When you are finished, jot down some observations in your journal.

Devotion 68

"There are six days when you may work, but the seventh day is a day of sabbath rest, a day of sacred assembly. You are not to do any work; wherever you live, it is a sabbath to the Lord."

LEVITICUS 23:3

Sabbath rest is built into the first days of creation, into the "appointed festivals" outlined by God in the Old Testament, and into the Ten Commandments. God does not give the impression that taking a Sabbath rest is optional.

Like with any rule, we can get a little bent out of shape because we don't like to be told what to do. Kind of like a kid throwing a tantrum about their bedtime. But rest is actually a luxurious gift from God. He doesn't want us working all the time, missing out on the fun. He wants us to enjoy life and be recharged, to spend time with him and with one another.

Jesus was confronted at times by some folks who thought the Sabbath was about rigid rules instead of rest—they didn't like that he was healing people or picking food to eat on the Sabbath. He responded that the Sabbath was made for people, not people for the Sabbath. It's not just a rule, it's a gift.

Practice You may have done quite a few practices from this book by now—mindfulness practices, meditations, and journal-writing. Notice if there is a practice that sounds restful for you right now. If so, take a moment to follow that practice. If not, give yourself permission to rest from your practice today and thank God for the gift of Sabbath rest.

The king covered his face and cried aloud, "O my
son Absalom! O Absalom, my son, my son!"

2 SAMUEL 19:4

King David grieved over the death of his son, Absalom. This is a bit surprising since Absalom had just spent several years conspiring to steal his father's throne. His death came as he was trying to kill his father, and yet his father's response was deep grief.

If you've ever wondered if you're allowed to feel a certain feeling, remember King David. He wasn't concerned about what emotion was right, he just expressed what he felt. The depth of his grief for Absalom was only made deeper by the loss of his son's loyalty, friendship, and trustworthiness over the years. So he let himself grieve hard, even when he got some backlash from the people who had just fought to defend him against his son's violent attack ("I see that you would be pleased if Absalom were alive today and all of us were dead," said his army commander in 2 Samuel 19:6 after killing Absalom to spare King David).

Is there something that you need to grieve? You don't need permission, and you don't need a reason. Just feel what you feel and God will carry you through, just like with King David.

Practice Following the working with difficulty guide on page 178–179, be present to any difficult emotions you might be experiencing such as grief, knowing that God carries you through. When you are finished, jot down some observations in your journal.

Devotion 70

Do not be stiff-necked, as your ancestors were; submit to the
LORD. Come to his sanctuary, which he has consecrated forever.

2 CHRONICLES 30:8

When you feel stressed or anxious, your body plays a big role in that, and one of the things you'll notice when you check in with your body is muscle tension. This is often manifested in a stiff, tight, or sore neck. Those muscles in the neck and shoulders can be like a gauge for our stress, letting us know just how much tension we're carrying around with us. (How's your neck now?)

Being "stiff-necked" has come to mean not just tight in our neck muscles, but also stubborn, resistant, proud, argumentative, hard-hearted, and unwilling to listen or to change. It's something that the Israelites got called a lot by God as they wandered around in the wilderness for forty years complaining and fighting him.

Meditation can be one way to loosen up your stiff neck—notice muscle tension, take a deep breath, smile, stretch. When you give yourself permission to let go of the tension in your body, you're giving yourself permission to let go of the tension in your mind as well. Being stiff-necked serves no purpose other than keeping you from joy and connection.

Practice Following the stretching/yoga practice on page 170–171, pay attention to the muscles in your neck as you move. Notice if there is an opportunity to let go of any tension, both in your body and in your mind. When you are finished, jot down some observations in your journal.

Devotion 71

*When I consider your heavens,/ the work of your fingers,/
the moon and the stars,/ which you have set in place,/ what
is mankind that you are mindful of them,/ human beings
that you care for them?/ You have made them a little lower
than the angels/ and crowned them with glory and honor.*

PSALM 8:3–5

Imagine God working the moon and stars into the heavens, setting them in place with his fingers like a sculptor or carpenter or gardener. And as the landscape of the universe comes together, imagine his fingers working you right into that beauty, right there below the angels, and then creating a crown for you of glory and honor.

Isn't this what we all want, to have glory (I am amazing and loved) and honor (I am respected and praised). And this is what you have. You have been woven into the beauty of the universe by the fingers of God himself, who holds you with the moon and stars and angels. You are amazing and loved. You are respected and praised.

This is not some future state. This is now, as God has created you. You are a part of God's glorious creation of the universe—never alone, a part of something so much bigger and more beautiful than you can even comprehend.

Practice Take some time today to look up at "the heavens," noticing the sky as part of God's handiwork (of which you are also a part). If you choose, write a brief prayer of gratitude in your journal for your place of honor in the created world.

Devotion 72

If you, LORD, kept a record of sins, / Lord, who could stand? / But with you there is forgiveness, / so that we can, with reverence, serve you.

PSALM 130:3–4

We all have an inner critic, and sometimes that critic can get noisy. Yours might keep you awake while you're trying to fall asleep ("That was a stupid thing I said."). It might try to talk you out of doing things you enjoy ("I'm not good at this."). It might keep you from taking healthy risks ("I'll probably fail.") or connecting with people who care about you ("They don't like me.").

But God does not talk to you like this. God is not keeping track of your mess-ups. God sees you as "righteous" because he sees you through the loving filter of forgiveness. When he listens to you, he smiles. When he looks at you, he sees his beautiful creation. There is no record of wrongs with God, because who could withstand such a brutal system? You can't be perfect and don't need to be.

The beautiful thing is that God's forgiveness means we can stop obsessing about ourselves and our performance and instead turn our eyes toward Jesus. God's forgiveness opens us up to joy, and it opens us up to worship and service. That's bad news for your inner critic, and that's really, really good news for your wellbeing.

Practice Following the lovingkindness/blessing guide on page 172–173, practice looking on yourself with compassion. You are loved. When you are finished, smile and write a prayer of receiving forgiveness in your journal.

Devotion 73

This is what the Sovereign LORD says to these bones: I will make breath enter you, and you will come to life.

EZEKIEL 37:5

You may have had times of feeling dead in your spirit—seasons of sadness or depression, or grief over the loss of someone (or something) important to you. You may even have responded to this heavy suffering with a loss of the desire to live.

God is all about restoring life. In this story, he gives the prophet Ezekiel a vision of dry bones, asking "Can these bones live?" While the most logical answer would have been no, God is all about life, and his answer was "yes." He attached tendons to the bones, added some flesh and skin, and breathed life into those dead bodies. And voilà, they were alive! A weird and also super cool metaphor for how serious God is about resurrection. Deadness is no match for him because he IS the breath of life.

You don't have to resurrect yourself when you're feeling dead or deflated. God will do that. You'll sometimes have to wait and hope, and you'll sometimes wonder if it's possible, but God is all about life (*your* life), and he will bring resurrection to pass.

 Practice Following the breathing space guide on page 176–177, notice the breath in your body which is God's breath, handed down since the beginning of human history. God is breathing life into you, and he will continue to do so. When you are finished, jot down some observations in your journal.

Devotion 74

*...After fasting forty days and forty nights, he was
hungry. The tempter came to him and said, "If you are
the Son of God, tell these stones to become bread."
Jesus answered, "It is written: 'Man shall not live on bread alone,
but on every word that comes from the mouth of God.'"*

MATTHEW 4:1–4

Jesus was SUPER hungry after fasting for 40 days. Satan urged
Jesus to ease his intense hunger quickly by turning stones into
bread, while also tempting him to give in to the thirst for power
and control with a miracle that would prove he was God.

Jesus could have ended his hunger right then and there, but
he would have been doing so as a knee-jerk reaction to temptation.

Instead, Jesus paused. He noticed the source of the urge,
which was the devil. He noticed the source of his life, which was
God ("Man shall not live on bread alone."). He chose not to grab
at the chance to prove himself and demonstrate his power, and he
waited. He was tempted again. And again. And then eventually,
"the devil left him, and angels came and attended him."

Are there hints about how you can work with your urges?

Practice Following the working with difficulty guide on
page 178–179, pay attention to urges that might tempt you to
quickly shut down discomfort. See if you can be intentional
about sticking with what is difficult for just a little bit longer,
resting in the knowledge that this too shall pass. When you
are finished, jot down some observations in your journal.

Devotion 75

*Peace I leave with you; my peace I give you. I do
not give to you as the world gives. Do not let your
hearts be troubled and do not be afraid.*

JOHN 14:27

The world dumps tough stuff on us, like violence, discrimination, and hatred. But Jesus doesn't give like this.

When Jesus left the earth in bodily form, he left the Holy Spirit behind, along with the gift of peace. Peace isn't something you have to find or manufacture. It's already inside of you because Jesus left it there as a going away present.

Of course, Jesus only went away in body. He is still with us in spirit, and this is why we're still able to access his lasting gift of peace. But it's an invisible gift (not like a birthday gift, wrapped up in a box), so it can be hard to figure out how to see it at times. Mindfulness meditation is one way to clear away the things the world gives so we can find the peace. It's a way of sorting out the trouble in our hearts so we can give up fear and open up to the peace of God that is left inside of us.

There is trouble in this world, and there's no way around that. But right alongside it is God's peace. Do not be afraid.

 Practice Following the breathing space guide on page 176–177, notice the build-up of troubles that the world has given as you take time to also notice the peace of God provided right alongside. When you are finished, jot down some observations in your journal.

Devotion 76

Early in the morning, Jesus stood on the shore, but the disciples did not realize that it was Jesus.

JOHN 21:4

Jesus had died in front of a huge crowd and been buried. Then he came to life and emerged from his sealed and guarded tomb. People knew he was alive again because he had started popping up but it turned out to be challenging for people to recognize him because they weren't expecting him.

Mary Magdalene thought Jesus was the gardener when he appeared to her in the garden outside of his tomb (until he said her name). And not too long later, his disciples saw him on the shore as they came back from a failed fishing trip and were oblivious to his identity (until he performed a miracle).

We, too, have trouble recognizing Jesus. We aren't watching for him, so when he shows up, we might miss him. We get so wrapped up in ourselves that we lose sight of God in our midst.

The good news is that once we recognize God, he is there waiting with celebration! When the disciples on the boat finally realized it was Jesus and scrambled to shore, Jesus cooked them a sunrise breakfast of fish and bread over a fire of burning coals. How cool is that?

Practice Following the centering prayer guide on page 184–185, practice noticing God with you. He is present and ready to connect. When you are finished, write a brief prayer in your journal acknowledging God and thanking him for showing up.

Devotion 77

All have sinned and fall short of the glory of God,
and all are justified freely by his grace through
the redemption that came by Christ Jesus.

ROMANS 3:23–24

Do you ever argue with someone in your head who isn't even there? The impulse to defend ourselves to the world is SO strong, whether our attacker is real or imaginary.

You don't have to prove yourself to anyone, and no one has to prove themselves to you. We're all sinners, and God has justified us. Freely. By his grace, because of Jesus.

So while being "justified freely by his grace" might sound like churchy mumbo-jumbo, stop for a minute and think what that means. You don't have to spend your energy defending yourself anymore. You can lay down the argumentative attempts to prove your worthiness. You can just smile at God and say "thanks—I needed that." Then see if there is something more fun you might like to spend your time doing besides argumentative circles in your own head, maybe even a way you can pass along some of that grace to another human. We're all in need of grace.

 Practice Following the walking/wheeling meditation guide on page 168–169, notice where your mind goes as you move. If arguments or defensive narratives arise, practice turning your attention back to the reality of God's grace. When you are finished, write a prayer of thanks in your journal for God's free forgiveness of all your mess-ups.

Devotion 78

We are surrounded by such a great cloud of witnesses . . .
let us run with perseverance the race marked out for us.

HEBREWS 12:1

The author of Hebrews tells about a host of people who kept the faith the best they knew how—Noah, Abraham, Jacob, Rahab, and others—and then described these as "witnesses" who surround us and inspire us to keep running our race with perseverance.

For an athlete, cheering crowds give energy and help to stay in the game even when the going gets tough. That encouragement is even more powerful when coming from someone who has been in the game before.

So many people have run this race of life before you, persevering through challenges as they root themselves in faith. None of them did it perfectly, but they are in Scripture because they kept coming back to God and trying again.

You might be able to think of some other "witnesses" from your family, community, or even the news. These people are all cheering you on, reminding you to persevere through the hard times so you can win the hard-earned prize at the end. You can do it!

Practice Write a list in your journal of people who have gone before you in the faith, creating a cloud of "witnesses" of your "race." This may include people that you know well and others that you have never met but you admire. Imagine this cloud of witnesses along the sidelines of your life, cheering you on as you persevere in the race.

Devotion 79

My dear brothers and sisters, take note of this:
Everyone should be quick to listen, slow to speak and
slow to become angry, because human anger does
not produce the righteousness that God desires.

JAMES 1:19–20

Angry feelings increase confidence and make it harder to take in information. Anger also speeds up reaction time—when you're mad, your brain can flare up quickly. So this guidance in Scripture is hard to practice. But psychology gives the same guidance for angry moments: Pause, listen, then react.

Anger itself is not bad—God himself demonstrates plenty of angry feelings throughout Scripture. But anger is kind of like fire. It serves a useful function but it needs to be handled carefully for safety reasons. When left completely unattended, anger can burn relationships and opportunities to the ground.

When you're angry, try pausing. Listen to yourself ("What do I want?"), to others ("What do they want?"), and to God ("What does God want?"). Then speak slowly and listen more.

Practice Bring to mind a situation where you feel angry toward someone. Answer the following questions. 1) Describe the situation and how it came about. 2) What do you want from the person and what are you getting? 3) What does the person want from you and what are they getting? 4) What physical sensations and emotions come with your anger? 5) What is your next step?

Devotion 80

But [the Lord] said to me, "My grace is sufficient for you, for my power is made perfect in weakness."... That is why, for Christ's sake, I delight in weaknesses, in insults, in hardships, in persecutions, in difficulties. For when I am weak, then I am strong.

2 CORINTHIANS 12:9–10

What are your weaknesses? After begging God to take his away, the Apostle Paul learned that his weaknesses were actually a container for God's power. When he stopped fighting against his weakness, he experienced God's strength.

You run into the limits of your weakness every day, because you're a human being. Learning to accept that as normal can free you up to live in God's strength. If you waste your time and energy wishing you didn't have weaknesses, it won't change the reality of your human limits. But if you smile at your weakness, you free up your energy to receive God's grace and provision.

Mindfulness practice gives you an opportunity to accept whatever is going on right now. This doesn't mean you have to like your weakness, it just means that you accept it is here. When you accept what is already here, you can open up to discover God's grace and strength that are perfectly sufficient, just like Paul.

Practice Following the walking/wheeling guide on page 168–169, notice any wobbling (or other "weakness") that is involved in moving forward or even in holding your body still. Notice how God is strengthening you, even as you experience weakness. When you are finished, jot down some observations in your journal.

Devotion 81

What good is it, my brothers and sisters, if someone claims to have faith but has no deeds?

JAMES 2:14

Are your deeds matching up with your faith? Aligning behavior with values is actually one predictor of mental health. None of us do this perfectly, but it's helpful to notice your patterns.

For example, if you believe that God is all-powerful and loving, are you practicing surrender of your worries to him each day? If you believe that we are called by Jesus to show compassion to everyone regardless of their social status, are you practicing kindness toward the classmate on the margins who needs a friend? If you believe that God's kingdom is more important than money, are you focusing as much on prayer as you are on seeking out the material things you want?

Turning our faith into deeds helps us experience the good of the Gospel, as we pass God's blessing to both others and ourselves. It lines up our values with our behavior. In the process, it supports our mental health and the health of our whole world.

What concrete step can you take today, however small, to match up your deeds with your faith?

Practice Following the lovingkindness/blessing guide on page 172–173, practice putting faith into action by blessing someone or receiving God's blessing yourself. When you are finished, set a goal of another way you will put your faith into action. Write it in your journal.

Devotion 82

*For here we do not have an enduring city, but we
are looking for the city that is to come.*

HEBREWS 13:14

Your family may have some keepsakes handed down from past generations—items that remind you of life lived by a deceased relative. As hard as you try to imagine exactly what life was like for that person, you will never be able to actually have the experience.

Even your own life moves quickly and experiences vanish quickly. An item bought on vacation can never take you back to a full version of that experience. It is over and never coming back.

Life and its experiences keep passing by, and eventually we are gone and the next generation takes over. Scripture reminds us to keep our eyes, then, on "the city that is to come." This life is just a blip in a much longer and fuller story than what we can see here.

When you make a beautiful sandcastle on the beach, you know the waves and wind will wash it away. But you build it anyway, and it's fun. Then you build one again at the next opportunity. This is life. Impermanent, always changing, ever-evolving, beautiful. Preparing us for the city that is to come.

Practice Following the sitting practice guide on page 167, pay attention to the impermanent, ever-changing nature of your experience. Each breath is new, each physical sensation is constantly changing, and all of this is part of the journey toward God's "city that is to come."

Devotion 83

Listen, my dear brothers and sisters: Has not God chosen those who are poor in the eyes of the world to be rich in faith and to inherit the kingdom he promised those who love him? But you have dishonored the poor.

JAMES 2:5–6

Honor is not often bestowed upon the poor. People experiencing homelessness can feel disrespected and lonely. People who cannot afford nice clothes can feel left out and judged. People who are left out of the political process can feel frustrated when those in power do not include their voice in decision-making.

Maybe you've had some of these experiences of feeling dishonored by others. It is almost always painful.

You have opportunities each day to show "honor" to "those who are poor in the eyes of the world." This is central to the gospel of Jesus—Christians laying aside stereotypes and biases against the poor, recognizing that God's call throughout Scripture is to honor the poor as heirs of the Kingdom. Given that we are all poor at different times in different ways, this is good news.

Mindfulness practice can be one way to pay attention to your thoughts about those the world dishonors, and to practice cultivating thoughts in your own mind that show honor toward the poor.

Practice Following the lovingkindness/blessing guide on page 172–173, turn your compassionate blessing toward someone who is experiencing poverty. Try honoring everyone you interact with throughout your day, whatever their position in society.

Devotion 84

. . . "I have had enough, Lord," he [Elijah] said. "Take my life; I am no better than my ancestors." Then he lay down under the bush and fell asleep. All at once an angel touched him and said, "Get up and eat." . . . He ate and drank and then lay down again.

1 KINGS 19:4–6

Elijah went through a lot for God, confronting evil governments and proving God's existence to the doubters through miraculous deeds. That got him into trouble with Queen Jezebel, who vowed to kill him. Elijah slumped into a depression, so despondent that he prayed to die. He was tired of the problems of life, of trying to do the right thing, of being on the run. He felt hopeless.

God's response to Elijah provides a good road map for us when life seems hopeless: a nap and a snack.

Your own strong emotions can often be calmed by sleeping or eating. And it's not just sleep and food, sometimes there are other practical kinds of self-care that are called for to move you through a slump—taking a walk, listening to a good song, meeting up with a trusted friend, writing in your journal.

Elijah is not the only one who needed these practical forms of self-care to continue on. How will you care for yourself today?

Practice Following the body scan guide on page 166, check in with your physical sensations without judging them. When you are finished, notice if there is any type of self-care that could help restore you as a next step. Then make a plan to implement that as a next step.

Devotion 85

And wherever he went—into villages, towns or countryside—they placed the sick in the marketplaces. They begged him to let them touch even the edge of his cloak, and all who touched it were healed.

MARK 6:56

Jesus often touched people to heal them, so sick people clamored to touch him as a way of receiving their healing.

Jesus isn't here with us in the flesh anymore, but he is with us in spirit and he continues to heal, sometimes through the sense of touch. God may have provided you with physical healing through the touch of a doctor's medical treatment or emotional healing through the touch of a loved one's hug in a sad moment. Or maybe you felt uplifted by the touch of warm sunshine on your face or refreshing water on your skin.

Another way God can use our sense of touch for healing can be mindfulness. When you pay full attention to what is coming through your sense of touch, you may notice contact, pressure, softness or hardness, smoothness or roughness, tingling, temperature, airflow, etc. Tuning into touch sensations directly can be one way to ground yourself in your body, restore your emotional equilibrium, and assess your physical needs in the moment. Try it out!

Practice Following the sensing guide on page 180–181, practice tuning in to your sense of touch by focusing on sensations on your skin. When you are finished, jot down some observations in your journal.

Devotion 86

Jesus asked them: "Why are you talking about having no bread? Do you still not see or understand? Are your hearts hardened? Do you have eyes but fail to see, and ears but fail to hear?"

MARK 8:17–18

Scripture sometimes calls us out about our difficulty using our eyes to actually see what God is up to. Jesus does this here, when right after he multiplied seven loaves into enough bread for four thousand people, his disciples started stressing out because they had forgotten to bring enough bread on their boat trip.

God is always providing for you, and he wants you to see it. This is a spiritual kind of seeing, but it's physical too, and you can access it through the physical act of seeing (or through your own way of physically perceiving the world, if you do not have access to eyesight).

Look around with your eyes and notice what comes in through your sense of sight. When you look at it directly (rather than just thinking about what you see or skimming over it to get to the next thing), you break some of the autopilot patterns in your thoughts and behaviors. You open up space to receive God's provision because you can see what he is up to, right in front of your eyes.

 Practice Following the sensing guide on page 180–181, practice paying attention to your sense of sight (colors, shapes, etc.), tuning into what is provided for you. When you are finished, jot down observations in your journal.

Devotion 87

And when he had taken it, the four living creatures and the twenty-four elders fell down before the Lamb. Each one had a harp and they were holding golden bowls full of incense, which are the prayers of God's people.

REVELATION 5:8

Good sci-fi gives us insight into the world as it actually is, with space age stories that get us thinking about real life themes.

The book of Revelation is a vision given by God to the Apostle John, and it reads like a good sci-fi story—it's full of dramatic imagery, horrifying creatures, violent conquests, and mysterious symbols. And it gives us insight into the world as it actually is.

In the image from this verse, we have golden bowls of incense, which are the prayers of God's people. Centuries before John recorded this vision, strong-smelling incense had been used to symbolize prayers rising up to God, and many churches today continue to use the smell of incense in this way.

What other smells does God provide to inspire you? Rain, cookies, flowers? Tuning into your sense of smell is one way to wake up to the vibrancy of God, and we can offer those smells back to God as worship, just like in the Apostle John's vision.

 Practice Following the sensing guide on page 180–181, tune into your sense of smell. You might select some pleasant fragrances (like lotion or a piece of fruit), or you might choose to just smell whatever is available. When you are finished, jot down some observations in your journal.

Devotion 88

Make every effort to live in peace with everyone and to be holy; without holiness no one will see the Lord. See to it that no one falls short of the grace of God and that no bitter root grows up to cause trouble and defile many.

HEBREWS 12:14–15

It's helpful that this verse starts with "make every effort," because living in peace with everyone and being holy definitely do not seem like things that are possible all the time.

Living in peace does NOT mean stuffing our feelings, putting on a happy face and pushing through anger and hurt as we try to please others. That's more like ignoring bitterness that just keeps growing the more we ignore it.

Good efforts at peace typically involve some conflict along the way, a willingness to work things out. Scary? Yes, sometimes. Effective at creating peace? Sometimes. But addressing conflict—and dealing with our bitter feelings—is a way of doing our best in cultivating peace from a place of honesty and wisdom.

Consider what your next step might be toward living in peace without being conflict-avoidant. Dealing with your bitter feelings now will mean more peace and less trouble in the long run.

Practice Bring to mind a situation where you feel some bitterness. Sit with that in God's presence for a few moments, accepting whatever you're feeling without judgment, noticing God's compassion for both you and the other person(s) involved. Then jot some notes in your journal.

Devotion 89

The Father . . . will give you another advocate to help you and be with you forever—the Spirit of truth. . . . You know him, for he lives with you and will be in you.

JOHN 14:16–17

Learning to quiet your inner critic is a lifelong process. The inner critic is that part of you that pretends to be motivating you but is actually just tearing you down by recycling unhelpful criticisms and lies about your worth. None of us are immune from this noisy enemy disguised as a friend.

Fortunately, God knows the truth about you and is on your side. One of the names for the Holy Spirit, in fact, is the Spirit of Truth—so we know that God is in the right about who you are and what your value is. Unlike that pesky inner critic, the goal of the Holy Spirit is actually to help you.

And this helping truth-teller lives in you and will be with you forever. This means you don't have to travel far to find the good truth about your worth. If you can get quiet enough to pay attention to yourself (using a compassionate tool like mindfulness) and then listen for God's truth (knowing that the Spirit of Truth is always with you), you will find help in quieting that noisy inner critic.

Practice Following the breathing space guide on page 176–177, pay attention to your experience with an awareness that your truth-telling friend, the Holy Spirit, is living in you and advocating for you right now (as always). You are loved. When you are finished, jot down some observations in your journal.

*. . . And after the fire came a gentle whisper. When Elijah
heard it, he pulled his cloak over his face and went
out and stood at the mouth of the cave. Then a voice
said to him, "What are you doing here, Elijah?"*

1 KINGS 19:12–13

God can be found in loud things at times, but not in this story.
Elijah had to wait through a hurricane, an earthquake, and a fire
before God showed up in a gentle whisper. Elijah responded by
covering his face and moving to the mouth of the cave. The first
thing God said in the quiet was "What are you doing here, Elijah?"

God will show up for you in the quiet too, and you may hear:
"What are you doing here?" It's a deep question that helps identify
your heart's greatest longing, your mind's most compelling goal,
your body's most important need. It's amazing that the God of the
universe wants to know your thoughts because it's very intimate.
Like any good conversation, answering this question will help you
know yourself and the questioner as well—God.

Don't answer the question too quickly. You need the waiting, the pause, the quiet, to get through the initial answers to the
deeper layer. "What are you doing here?"

Practice Following the centering prayer guide on page
184–185, spend some time in the quiet with God. Notice any
longings that come up, as you repeatedly bring your attention back to God's presence. When you are finished, write a
brief prayer of response in your journal.

Devotion 91

*There is a time for everything,/ and a season for every
activity under the heavens:/ . . . a time to weep and a
time to laugh,/ a time to mourn and a time to dance.*

ECCLESIASTES 3:1, 4

You've had some friendships come and go. You've had some awesome experiences end while others begin. Maybe you've moved or changed schools. Maybe you've experienced major loss in your life that knocked you down, and maybe you've had other seasons that felt super fun. The only constant thing in life is change.

Your emotions change all the time, just like everything else. When you're happy, you might think life will always be great; when you're down, you might think you'll always feel depressed.

Mindfulness teaches you to view your emotions like changing weather rather than permanent states. Feelings can be interesting to watch, in the same way we watch thunderstorms, sunny skies, tornadoes, and crisp autumn days. This viewpoint can allow you to be less judgmental toward feelings and more curious about them. Watching them come and go like clouds means that you're not grabbing onto unpleasant feelings to fight them—you're simply watching the emotional storm clouds build, hover, dump their rain, and pass. You're getting out of God's way as he brings the next new thing.

Practice Following the mountain meditation guide on page 174–175, notice any changes that might occur in your emotions throughout the practice, no matter how slight. When you are finished, jot down some observations in your journal.

Devotion 92

*By faith we understand that the universe was
formed at God's command, so that what is seen
was not made out of what was visible.*

HEBREWS 11:3

Look around. Everything you see was made out of the invisible.
While scientists continue to work on understanding how this is
possible, God already knows because he brought everything into
being from nothing.

Take a moment to look at one object in front of you. Imagine
the materials that it is made out of being formed. Everything is
made from something else, something that God already created
out of nothing. It would be weird if there was nothing in front of
you and then suddenly a chair appeared—but that's really how it
was. There was nothing, and then by God's command the universe
was formed.

We take the universe we live in for granted because we're used
to seeing it. But it can look a lot different when we imagine God
bringing each piece of it into being from nothing.

Practice Following the eating meditation guide on page
182–183, notice how God commanded this particular food
into existence for your nourishment and pleasure. Where
there was previously invisible nothingness, he spoke into
being the materials to make up this piece of food for you to
take into your body at this particular time. When you are
finished, jot down some observations in your journal.

Devotion 93

The grace of the Lord Jesus be with God's people. Amen.

REVELATION 22:21

Have you read the stories of God's people in the Bible? They were a mess. A lot of the most revered people in Scripture made pretty horrific mistakes. Maybe you haven't killed anyone like many of the Biblical "saints" did, but your life has its own messiness.

God's people aren't perfect people (since there aren't any of those). We're people who know we've messed up and continue coming back to God for grace, and then God uses us in surprising ways that point other people to God. Sometimes it's the enormity of our mistakes that leads us to "hit rock bottom" and come crawling back to God.

When you feel like a mess, know that this blessing found at the very end of the Bible (and all throughout as well) is just for you. It's grace. You, as one of God's people, are given grace as God's last word in Scripture. Like all of the saints who have gone before, your mess is made clean by God's grace. You'll mess up again, and God knows that. Just be ready to crawl back to him again and receive his grace. All is forgiven.

Practice Following the stretching/yoga guide on page 170–171, notice what feels good for your body during this gentle exercise and receive that as grace. When you are finished, write a brief prayer in your journal of receiving God's offered grace in the midst of life's mess, if you choose.

Devotion 94

Above all else, guard your heart,
for everything you do flows from it.

PROVERBS 4:23

Your heart is like the source of a spring—from a fresh spring will flow fresh water, and from a well-tended heart will come a life well-tended. Everything you do flows from your heart.

When we guard our hearts, it's not with the intention of keeping out the good stuff. Quite the opposite. You can carefully stand guard against the dangerous attacks of lies, oppression, bigotry, and self-condemning thoughts. But a good heart-guard will allow in the heart's safe friends, perhaps best summed up in Galatians 5:22–23 as "the fruit of the Spirit"—love, joy, peace, patience, kindness, goodness, faithfulness, gentleness, and self-control. These qualities fill your heart with good things, and then good things flow out of your life to others as well.

You are not meant to choose between caring for yourself and caring for others. Guard your own wellbeing, protecting your heart and showing it kindness. Let in the good and then release that goodness to share freely with others.

Practice Focus your attention on your breath moving in and out. With each out-breath, imagine you are breathing out unpleasant emotions and thoughts. With each in-breath, imagine you are breathing God's care into the center of your heart. In this way, you are guarding your heart, inviting in the fruit of the Spirit to nourish you and others.

Devotion 95

And our hope for you is firm, because we know that just as you share in our sufferings, so also you share in our comfort.

2 CORINTHIANS 1:7

An old proverb says "A grief shared is a grief halved. A joy shared is a joy doubled." While the math here might vary from one situation to another, the basic principle is solid—sharing your joys and sorrows makes life better.

Being independent is great, but it's not the end-all-be-all. It doesn't produce happiness. Research shows that happiness is bolstered by social connection. Even with all the challenges of getting along with friends and family, God wired our positive emotions to be fueled by belonging with others.

Who do you share your joys and sorrows with? Where is your community? If you're not sure, no worries—it takes a while sometimes to find our people. But don't give up, because God wants a caring community for you, a place where you can be your true self and share life. It's one of the ways you'll get through the hard times and make the most of the joyful times.

Practice Following the lovingkindness/blessing guide on page 172–173, bring to mind a caring person with whom you share your joys and sorrows (or someone with whom you would like to create such a connection). As you repeat the prayer of compassionate blessing, allow yourself to rest in emotional connection. When you are finished, jot down some observations in your journal.

Devotion 96

"The word is near you; it is in your mouth and in your heart."

ROMANS 10:8

A popular song in the 1990s told us that "God is watching us from a distance." These lyrics were woefully incomplete. God is not just watching you from a distance, because God is also right here with you, as close as your breath. His word is so near that this verse describes it as being "in your mouth and in your heart." You can't really have God any closer than that.

It's cool that the God who is within you and surrounding you is also present to the ends of the universe at distances greater than our human brains can fathom. When you breathe in, you are breathing into this very space that God is, and this connects you to the vast universe that God indwells.

We can practice paying attention to the nearness of God. We can notice that he is here, putting his words of love and compassion into our hearts and mouths. When you notice how near you are to God, you have a chance of noticing your true identity as a child of God—connected, compassionately cared for, and created as part of this beautiful universe.

Practice Following the centering prayer guide on page 184–185, practice returning your attention (over and over) to the presence of God—notice how near God is to you right now. When you are finished, see if it is possible to bring this awareness of God's nearness with you into the rest of your day.

Devotion 97

"Martha, Martha," the Lord answered, "you are worried and upset about many things, but few things are needed—or indeed only one. Mary has chosen what is better, and it will not be taken away from her."

LUKE 10:41–42

This story highlights two sisters—generously hospitable Martha and fully present Mary. Martha hosts Jesus and his disciples in her home. But she is "upset about many things." Her feelings of distraction and anxiety lead her to snap at her sister.

As Martha is bustling around to prepare a meal for the large group in her home, Mary is sitting at Jesus' feet, listening to him. It's not hard to empathize with Martha's frustration here—she feels uncared for by Jesus and Mary, ignored and taken advantage of. But when she expresses this, Jesus sides with Mary.

It appears that Martha's distraction, despite being connected to her generosity, ended up distracting her from the most important thing. Jesus was there, a miracle-worker who could have created a meal for them out of nothing. Martha fell into the worrisome trap of thinking human effort was what was needed, when in reality it was God that was needed. And God was in the room.

Practice Following the stretching/yoga guide on page 170–171, notice any unnecessary striving in your practice. Could it be that you could go a bit easier on yourself as you receive God's provision in this moment? When you are finished, write a prayer of "letting go" in your journal.

Devotion 98

*Then the L*ORD *God formed a man from the dust of
the ground and breathed into his nostrils the breath
of life, and the man became a living being.*

GENESIS 2:7

At the beginning of human history, God made a person and breathed into his nostrils "the breath of life." That's what made that first man a living being instead of a blob of dust—God's breath in his lungs. When the next human was fashioned as a woman, she had the capacity (along with the male) to reproduce more humans, and every generation since those first two people have passed down what God first gave to Adam—God's breath.

Whatever your relationship with your biological parents, God used them and all the relatives before them to pass along that divine breath to you. Each living baby emerging from their mother's womb takes a big gulp of breath. Their loud cry lets us know they are healthy and alive as they receive God's breath of life. God's breath will continue moving through their lungs until their dying day.

When you breathe, are you aware that you are breathing God's breath, handed down from the beginning of time?

Practice Following the breathing space guide on page 176–177, notice that the breath in your lungs was breathed by God himself, passed down through your long line of ancestors to you. When you are finished, write a brief prayer in your journal of receiving that breath, if you choose.

Devotion 99

Let no one deceive you with empty words.

EPHESIANS 5:6

There are SO MANY WORDS in our modern era—so much input from so many people across so many screens and audio systems. Many of these are from people trying to get something from you. Whether these words are seeking access to your money, attention, approval, or sex, they are so often deceitful and empty.

There are also honest and "full" words out there—words that support your wellbeing and personal growth, pointing you toward a loving God and grounding you in truth. These words are not manipulative and they do not leave you wounded or hollow. They fill you up, like a good meal.

Pay careful attention to the words you hear. What are they asking of you, and is it good for your soul? How do you feel (short term and long term) when you hear them? Are these life-giving words that you would pass along to someone you respect and admire? Asking these kinds of questions will help you avoid being deceived by empty words.

Practice Pay attention to the word input in your life today. Whether from shows, music, texts (or other communications), social media, articles, or other sources, practice awareness of when words are deceitful and empty or when they are honest and full. Pay attention to the impact on you, and then take some time to write down observations about this in your journal.

Devotion 100

Even the very hairs of your head are all numbered.

MATTHEW 10:30

Counting your hairs would be pretty tricky, so it's amazing to think that God knows the number of hairs on everyone's head. That's a very specific level of detail about our physical bodies! God knows everything there is to know about you. Whether you find that comforting or a little frightening, it's the way it is.

It turns out that numbering things can sometimes be used as a mental health tool. For example, it can be calming to quietly and slowly count breaths while you sit still. A related technique is called square breathing, which involves counting to 4 on an in-breath, holding your breath to the count of 4, and repeating on an out-breath.

Breathing techniques like this can tune you into the rhythm of your body breathing, helping you notice the things about you that God is already aware of. He created your body—your hair, breath, every detail of your physical existence. He knows the numbers. He knows you well, and he loves you.

Practice Decide between the two breath-counting techniques described above, then set a timer for anywhere from one to three minutes. Close your eyes (either halfway or all the way—whatever you're comfortable with) and engage with the practice until your timer goes off. When you are finished, write a brief reflection in your journal regarding God's knowledge of your body's details.

Devotion 101

"Wake up, sleeper,/ rise from the dead,/
and Christ will shine on you."

EPHESIANS 5:14

Waking up in the morning can be tough, but so can staying awake to our lives in general. Ways you might be tempted to "sleep" through your life include keeping your earbuds in, avoiding social situations, staring at your phone, overthinking, or just not paying attention. Without the right balance of rest and activity, we grow lethargic and shut down. We feel less happy and alive.

God encourages us to wake up, to be aware! You've been given one life to live. It would be sad to reach the end and realize you avoided the good stuff because you were disconnected, avoidant, or zoned out. Even though being awake involves discomfort, it also gives you access to those experiences that bring joy, connection, and meaning. You might feel anxious about going to that youth group meeting or taking that solo hike in nature, but experiences like that will keep your soul alive and open you up to receive the light of Christ in your heart.

Get some sleep then wake up and be present!

 Practice Following the guide for the sensing guide on page 180–181, choose one sense to focus on and set a timer for at least one minute. Use the practice to "wake up" to what is coming into your sensory experience and be curious about what God is providing right now. When you are finished, jot down some observations in your journal.

Devotion 102

"For my thoughts are not your thoughts,/ neither are your ways my ways,"/ declares the LORD.

ISAIAH 55:8

When a child wants a bucket of candy at the store, they might throw a tantrum when their parent doesn't agree. The parent is thinking "I want my child to have a healthy body and mind. Saying no is in their best interest." The child is thinking "My parent is so mean and unfair."

The parent is using reasonable thinking in this situation, with the good of their child at heart. But we all know that candy tastes really good and it's normal to want it, even when it's unreasonable.

God says that we're kind of like that child in the store—our thoughts generally seem true and reality-based. But God is like the parent who wants us to be healthy and well and sees the bigger picture. He does fill our life with good things, but there will be moments of suffering and disappointment. We can trust that even when things don't make sense to us, they make sense to God.

Practice Set a timer for 3 minutes, close your eyes (if you choose), and start to notice your thoughts. See them as events happening in your mind that do not need a response. Imagine that God is smiling at you, and notice that God's thoughts are different than yours—you don't know what they are, but you know he's seeing the whole picture and has your good at heart. When you are finished, write a brief prayer of surrender to God in your journal, if you choose.

Devotion 103

Hope does not put us to shame, because God's love has been poured out into our hearts through the Holy Spirit.

ROMANS 5:5

You have blood moving through your body all the time, constantly pumped through your arteries and veins by your heart. So imagine for a minute God pouring love into your ever-pumping heart. As your heart moves your blood, it moves God's love right along with it, all the way through you, keeping you alive. Your body is being constantly supplied and resupplied with blood—and also with love.

This is what Scripture says has happened—God has poured love into your heart. There's not a part of you that is not being supplied with the love of God. And this is why there is hope. Not because of anything you have done (although you've done cool stuff) and not because good things will happen in the future (although they will). Hope is present just because of the love, poured into your heart by God and then consistently supplied to all of who you are by that continuously pumping heart.

Practice Following the sitting practice guide on page 167, focus your attention on any sensations of your heart beating that you can detect (along with the lungs breathing on either side of your heart). See if you're able to detect any sensations of blood flow or pulsing throughout your body, perhaps in your feet or limbs. Notice that God's love is flowing through you as well. When you are finished, jot down some observations in your journal.

Devotion 104

There is now no condemnation for those
who are in Christ Jesus.

ROMANS 8:1

You may struggle to accept yourself, but Jesus does not. You may harshly criticize yourself, but Jesus does not. You may wonder if you are likable, but Jesus does not. In Jesus, there is no condemnation.

If you don't like how you look, sound, or act, rest assured that these "condemning" thoughts in your head are not "facts" about you, and neither are the insecure feelings that come with them. God gets to name reality as it really is, and God has clearly said that you are covered by grace.

What does it mean to be "in Christ Jesus?" Really just that you've said yes to Jesus' grace. You've decided to orient your life around the way of Jesus and you've chosen to receive the beautiful gift of non-condemnation. Granted, you will need to receive that gift over and over and over, but that's the beauty of God's forgiveness and grace. It's always available, whenever we're ready to set down the heavy weight of condemnation once again so our hands are available to receive his grace. Now that's a swap worth making.

Practice Following the body scan guide on page 166, practice setting aside judgment to observe your body without condemnation. If you notice harsh thoughts toward yourself, set those free to God's care as you receive his love and grace. When you are finished, jot down some observations in your journal.

Devotion 105

I say to myself, "The LORD is my portion;
therefore I will wait for him."

LAMENTATIONS 3:24

A portion is a serving. It is the right amount, enough to provide you with what you need.

You might be used to thinking you'll get enough of what you need when things change in the future. A person can go through high school thinking that they'll have enough when they're in college, and then when they have a job after college, and then when they get married, and then when they have children, and then when they're empty nesters, and then when they retire, and then . . . It's a sad thought to think of getting to the end of life with the realization that you were always waiting for something else to bring you fulfillment and happiness, for something different to feel like enough.

God says that he is your portion, he is enough. That means that being present in this moment with God is where you will find what you need, because God is enough. In those inevitable places where you feel lacking or longing, God will provide and in fact is already providing right now. You have everything you need.

Practice Following the working with difficulty guide on page 178–179, notice any tendency to push away what is difficult in hopes of something better. Notice God's provision in the moment. You are provided with enough of what you need to care well for your difficulty in this moment. When you are finished, jot down observations in your journal.

Devotion 106

For we do not have a high priest who is unable to empathize with our weaknesses, but we have one who has been tempted in every way, just as we are—yet he did not sin. Let us then approach God's throne of grace with confidence, so that we may receive mercy and find grace to help us in our time of need.

HEBREWS 4:15–16

Knowing you are not alone is important for your wellbeing. This is why therapy groups work so well, and why you may find yourself drawn to people who have lived experiences similar to your own.

This is one of the things that makes God awesome. He has lived similar experiences to yours, and he gets you. While on earth, Jesus went through lots of really hard things, including physical torture and death. He also went through temptation "in every way, just as we are"—he knows how hard it is to walk away from things that feel good now but hurt in the long run.

And like a good friend or fellow group therapy participant, Jesus is empathic and not judgmental about your weaknesses. He uses his own earthly experiences to say "It's really tough—I get it." This serves as an invitation for you to approach his throne with confidence, knowing that there is mercy and grace available when we need it.

Practice Following the walking/wheeling guide on page 168–169, notice you are walking or wheeling across the same earth Jesus walked. You are following in his footsteps, encountering difficulty as he did but also not alone as he was. When you are finished, jot down some observations in your journal.

Devotion 107

Then God said, "I give you every seed-bearing plant on the face of the whole earth and every tree that has fruit with seed in it. They will be yours for food."

Genesis 1:29

It often seems as if food appears from nowhere. Perhaps you've grown some of your own food, but chances are much of your food is taken off a store shelf and plopped in a grocery cart without thought about its origins. You may not even know what ingredients are in much of your food, or where they came from.

When you bite into a vegetable or fruit, do you imagine the plant on which it grew? If you eat meat, do you imagine the living animal from which it was taken? When you eat processed food, are you aware of the many complicated-sounding ingredients?

Everything you eat comes somehow from the earth, and God put it there. You can pick an apple straight from the tree or you can harvest multiple sources of food and process them before mixing them together, but either way, you are eating what God has given you for food. Your physical nourishment matters to God.

Practice Identify one food you have eaten in the past day, then use your journal to list all the places to which this food can be traced back in its original state. Or if you would prefer, follow the eating meditation guide on page 182–183 to increase awareness of your food's sources. Then write a prayer in your journal of thanksgiving to God for providing you with the sources of this food, if you choose.

Devotion 108

Jesus Christ is the same yesterday and today and forever. Do not be carried away by all kinds of strange teachings. It is good for our hearts to be strengthened by grace, not by eating ceremonial foods, which is of no benefit to those who do so.

HEBREWS 13:8–9

The gospel of Christ is pretty straightforward—people sin (hurting ourselves and one another), so we all deserve punishment. But God loves us so much that he chose to live on earth as a human for a while and to take the punishment we deserve through death. Now we are forgiven through grace! Our part is to say yes to that grace and to follow in Christ as much as we can.

The author of Hebrews knew that people were making the gospel more complicated with "strange teachings" related to food and faith. We have the same problem now, with lots of strange teachings about faith, food, relationships, and everything else. So this reminder is for you too—keep it simple. Your strength comes from God's grace, not from following complicated rules or performing well.

You are loved, forgiven, and accepted through Jesus, and that will never change. Allow your heart to be strengthened by that simple truth of the gospel today.

Practice Following the centering prayer guide on page 184–185, notice that God is present with you—the same God who has been present throughout history is here now, strengthening your heart with grace. When you are finished, write a prayer of gratitude to God for simple grace in your journal.

Devotion 109

There is no one righteous, not even one . . . for all
have sinned and fall short of the glory of God.

ROMANS 3:10, 23

It's probably not hard to list ways that the people in your life have fallen short and how you would like them to be different. You are conscious of your own flaws as well, aware of the gap between you and your ideal self.

God agrees that we all fall short. Not even one of us is righteous, and we certainly do not have the kind of "glory" that God displays. While celebrities may seem perfect even they are regular people with difficult issues in their real lives.

Knowing this about our human condition can give us compassion for one another. It's really hard to be human, and we all struggle to be the people we want to be. You will often not act the way you wish you could act, and that is painful. The same is true for those around you, even those extra-difficult people that you know.

Consider practicing some compassion toward a difficult person in your life today. Don't allow them to mistreat you (boundaries are important!), but you may find some softness in your heart as you consider that they need compassion, just like you.

Practice Following the lovingkindness/blessing guide on page 172–173, identify a difficult person toward whom you can practice extending compassion. If that is painful, be sure to extend plenty of compassion toward yourself as well. When you are finished, jot down some observations in your journal.

Devotion 110

Finally, brothers and sisters, whatever is true, whatever is noble, whatever is right, whatever is pure, whatever is lovely, whatever is admirable—if anything is excellent or praiseworthy—think about such things.

PHILIPPIANS 4:8

When people want to get your attention, they will often use anxiety-provoking messages. The advertising world and the news cycle keep you hooked by making you feel anxious about yourself and your world so you keep returning to their products.

Because of this, it takes extra work to notice the good stuff. The kind words, the compassionate gestures, the peaceful resolution of conflict between people, the beautiful things in the natural world. The list could go on and on—there is SO much in the world that is right, pure, lovely, admirable, excellent, and praiseworthy.

God encourages us to take time to think about these good things. This doesn't take away life's hard stuff, but you can dilute the pain of the hard things by expanding your attention to include the good things. A teaspoon of salt tastes nasty if you drink it in a small cup of water, but if you mix it in a barrel of water you won't even taste it. So it is with our attention—if you can expand your attention to include the good, it has a diluting effect on the bad.

Practice Use your journal to list some "excellent" things in the world. You don't have to feel any certain way, but see if you can savor the good for a bit, and then carry that awareness with you into the rest of your day.

Devotion 111

*Whoever finds their life will lose it, and whoever
loses their life for my sake will find it.*

MATTHEW 10:39

Let it be. Let it go. These are phrases popularized by famous songs, but the concept is still really hard. Our more natural tendency is more along the lines of "make it change; don't release your grip."

Long before modern pop singers got to these phrases though, Jesus was already preaching letting go. Lose your life, he said. What in the world could he have meant by that?

Holding your life loosely is helpful for mental health because you'll be less attached to expectations and more adaptable through life's inevitable surprises and disappointments. It's also helpful for your spiritual life, shifting your attention to be less self-focused and more open to God's leading.

Keep moving toward your goals and dreams, but be ready to let them go when God shows you something even better. His way may be unexpected and surprising, and it may even seem like a raw deal at first. But rest assured that giving up how you think your life is supposed to be will, in the end, set you free to find the good life that God has for you.

 Practice Following the stretching/yoga guide on page 170–171, notice any tension you're holding on to in your body or any way that you think your body is supposed to be during the practice. Then practice letting it go through movement. When you are finished, jot down some observations in your journal.

Devotion 112

"Whoever has ears to hear, let them hear."

MARK 4:9

If you have access to your sense of hearing, take a minute to pause and listen to sounds around you. Chances are that you are now picking up on a few sounds you didn't notice before. Your brain tunes out most sounds so that you don't get too distracted or over-stimulated by trying to process too many sounds at once.

Unfortunately, we also tune out much of what God is saying to us. Jesus says that if you have ears, you should use them. And he said this after sharing the Parable of the Sower, referring to the ways you might hear with your ears but also with your heart and mind and soul.

When you practice hearing, you are practicing really paying attention to what is going on. You can start to pick up things you didn't notice before. Sometimes these will just be noises. Sometimes they will be new insights. Sometimes they will be words from God. But it all starts with truly hearing what is going on—hearing with your ears, your heart, your mind, and your soul.

 Practice Following the sensing guide on page 180–181, tune into your sense of hearing. As much as hearing is accessible to you, notice the sounds around you and be curious about what might come to your awareness as you truly pay attention. When you are finished, jot down some observations in your journal.

*If anyone will not welcome you or listen to your words,
leave that home or town and shake the dust off your feet.*

MATTHEW 10:14

Jesus sent his disciples out to preach the good news and heal people with God's authority. "Freely you have received; freely give," he said. But he clarified this important instruction—if someone does not want your preaching or healing, move on. Don't remain stuck in a toxic relationship cycle. Keep moving, because you can find people who are more welcoming and ready to listen.

Do you have any relationships where you are being consistently hurt, rejected, or ignored? How about relationships where you are trying to help but the other person just isn't accepting your help or treating you well? These can be very difficult situations, and trying too hard for too long can sometimes leave us stuck and wounded. You may want to talk with a trusted person in your life about whether it is wise to step away. Jesus doesn't want you stuck in a toxic relationship.

Practice Bring to mind a relationship that is difficult for you. In a spirit of prayerfulness, answer the following questions in your journal. 1) Describe the difficult relationship. 2) What do you want from the person and what do you actually get? 3) What does the person want from you and what do they actually get? 4) What do you feel emotionally in regards to this relationship? 5) Is the difficulty resolved now? If not, what is your next step?

Devotion 114

"Here is a boy with five small barley loaves and two small fish, but how far will they go among so many?"

JOHN 6:9

God provides enough for us, but we often don't see it. This is what happened in the story of Jesus feeding a huge crowd. It seemed obvious to the disciples that there wasn't enough food, and they scoffed at the silliness of even paying attention to the boy's small amount of bread and fish in the midst of such overwhelming need.

But paying attention to that small amount was exactly what Jesus asked of his disciples. He took the small amount of food, said a grateful prayer, and distributed it to person after person in the crowd until everyone was fed.

When you're feeling deprived, do you notice the clothes on your back, the chair you're sitting in, and the food you have eaten? When you're feeling ignored, do you notice the small smile someone gives you in passing? When you're feeling bored, do you notice the amazing and brightly colored bug slowly crawling on the step outside? We are surrounded by small things that are ready for God's miracles of multiplication, if only we will pay attention.

Practice Following the sitting guide on page 167, notice any ways that your thoughts wander into a "not enough" mentality. Practice an awareness of whatever you are experiencing in the moment as a way to be present for God's miracle of "enough." When you are finished, jot down some observations in your journal.

Devotion 115

"In repentance and rest is your salvation,/ in quietness and trust is your strength,/ but you would have none of it."

ISAIAH 30:15

Being quiet and restful is not always at the top of our agenda, but this is where God says we get our strength. Repenting of the notion that we run the world frees us up for a more trusting relationship with our maker.

Will you accept this offer from God to be quiet and restful in order to recharge your strength? If you're a person who likes to keep moving, it may take some shifting of your priorities. You might also find it uncomfortable to be still as you become more aware of your thoughts and feelings. You'll have to take your defenses down for a bit to actually deal with the stuff you've been avoiding.

It's this letting down of your defenses that gives you a chance to be vulnerable with God. When you do that, he will strengthen you. Working quiet into your daily program will help you be charged for all the other things you have going on. Don't be one of those people who "would have none of it" when God offers you rest.

Practice Take a moment for quiet rest using this Take Five grounding exercise. Slowly notice 5 things you can see, 4 things you can hear, 3 things you can feel with your skin, 2 things you can smell, and 1 thing you can taste. See if you can experience each directly (instead of thinking about them) as you ground yourself in the present moment.

Devotion 116

Therefore we do not lose heart. Though outwardly we are wasting away, yet inwardly we are being renewed day by day.

2 CORINTHIANS 4:16

Some things are challenging, whether they relate to family, relationships, health, or academics. This may have led to times when you felt you were "wasting away," physically or emotionally.

Both Scripture and psychology teach us that we can nurture wellbeing in the midst of difficult circumstances. Heroes of the faith have demonstrated this. Maybe you've heard of Corrie ten Boom, whose witness to the gospel grew stronger in reaction to the torture she endured in a Nazi concentration camp. Or Joni Erickson Tada who has used a life-altering spinal cord injury to spread love and hope to others in similar situations.

This does not mean that you must feel happy all the time or fake joy during tough times. But it means that you have an opportunity to care for your heart in a way that allows you to be renewed through the trials.

Mindfulness practices are one way to connect with that calm center in your heart that is experiencing renewal. Take time to pay attention to your inside—the part of you that God is refreshing and renewing every day, even at this moment.

 Practice Following the sitting practice on page 167, notice that your heart center is being constantly renewed even in the midst of whatever is happening in your life. When you are finished, jot down some observations in your journal.

I remain confident of this:
I will see the goodness of the LORD
in the land of the living.

PSALM 27:13

Life's badness can be easier to see than its goodness at times. The headlines tell us of non-stop tragedy and doom around the world, and your vision of your own life may be similarly skewed at times.

The good is still there all the time though because God is good all the time. Do you know how to see it? It takes practice.

You can start by rewriting the headlines. What if your news stream today highlighted events like "sunrise this morning includes five shades of pink" and "old man receives compassionate care from nursing attendant" and "baby's smile awakens joy in many hearts." Or perhaps it would highlight the comfort of a warm drink, the excitement of a long-anticipated trip, or the whisper of God's comfort in a sorrowful moment.

We can be confident that if we look for goodness, we will see it. The challenge is not whether good exists, but whether we can be aware of it. Here in the land of the living, the Lord is giving us good things, if only we have the eyesight to see them.

Practice Following the body scan on page 166, notice your body as a way of seeing God's goodness here "in the land of the living." When you are finished, jot down some observations in your journal.

✧ⁱ☆ⁿ✶ *Devotion 118* ✖ⁱⁱ☆⁼

"In me you may have peace. In this world you will have
trouble. But take heart! I have overcome the world."

JOHN 16:33

The catchy song "Don't Worry, Be Happy" lists a random assortment of troubles: you can't afford your rent, you're not in a relationship, your bed has been stolen, you are lacking fashion sense. But the songwriter offers the same advice for all: "Don't worry, be happy."

Jesus also encourages you to shift your focus off your troubles and recognize that he has overcome the world and offers peace. Your troubling circumstances do not define you or your happiness.

Do you know how to connect with that place of God's peace within you, no matter the circumstance? It's no easy feat, but it's part of Jesus' offer to you. He overcomes your troubles and provides peace. Your part is to practice connecting with it.

Mindfulness practices are one way to slow down enough to connect your heart with God's peace. You don't have to force any particular feeling, but getting out of your head and into the present moment is one way to make space for peace.

Practice Following the body scan on page 166, practice shifting your thoughts from a focus on troubles to your physical sensations in the moment. Notice what it feels like to practice less attachment to thinking about your troubles and more awareness of what is happening in your body (there are no thoughts in your belly!). When you are finished, jot down some observations in your journal.

Devotion 119

"Forget the former things;/ do not dwell on the past./ See, I am doing a new thing!/ Now it springs up; do you not perceive it?/ I am making a way in the wilderness/ and streams in the wasteland.

Isaiah 43:18–19

What percentage of your mental activity is occupied with rehashing the past? Probably a decent amount. Can you imagine how much more mental space you would have without that?

When you dwell on the past, you give up control over the present because your mind is stuck on something that cannot be changed. Some debriefing of the past is helpful, but mindless looping of thoughts about the past does not tend to help us heal, learn, or grow.

God invites you to pay attention to what is happening now. The prophet Isaiah said where there is wilderness, God is making a way for you. Where there is a wasteland, he is creating streams of water. But it's not hard to miss this present-moment stuff when you are dwelling on the past. This is why God asks "Do you not perceive it?" Oftentimes, the answer is "Actually no, I totally missed that thing happening right now because I was lost in my thoughts about the past."

Learning to pay attention to the present moment will help you notice God's provision in your life.

 Practice Following the breathing space guide on page 176–177, practice noticing what is here in the present moment. God is doing something new. Can you perceive it? When you are finished, jot down some observations in your journal.

Devotion 120

Jesus said, "Peace be with you! As the Father has sent me, I am sending you." And with that he breathed on them and said, "Receive the Holy Spirit."

JOHN 20:21–22

God has used breath for quite a few things throughout the history of the world, including imparting the Holy Spirit by breathing on his disciples. He didn't just use words or outstretched hands, he literally breathed on them. God's breath empowered those first disciples to go out into the world as representatives of God and to carry God's Spirit within them. That's big stuff.

This is a clue about the power of that breath coming in and out of your lungs right now. Each breath connects you back to the creation of the world when God breathed into the first human. Each connects you to the Holy Spirit. And paying attention to each breath also has the power to calm you, ground you, and center you. God uses breath to create a soothing rhythm inside of our bodies that is always present and always available.

When you need to remember that God is with you and you are okay, try paying attention to your breath.

Practice One way to help focus attention on your breath is square breathing, in which you count to 4 on an inhale, hold to 4, count to 4 on an exhale, hold to 4, and repeat. Try out this approach to breath awareness as you sit in the presence of God who is the giver of all breath. When you are finished, jot down some observations in your journal.

Devotion 121

Now to him who is able to do immeasurably more than all we ask or imagine, according to his power that is at work within us, to him be glory in the church and in Christ Jesus throughout all generations, for ever and ever! Amen.

EPHESIANS 3:20–21

You probably have some ideas about how things should be different than they are. It's hard to get through a day without multiple reminders that things are not as they are supposed to be.

Sin creates walls between people, as well as between us and our own goals. You can spend your time wishing this weren't the case and getting angry about all the ways people are messing up. But this is kind of like beating your head against the wall of reality. It doesn't change reality, and it makes your head hurt.

Rather than focusing all your attention on how things should be, try this instead—accept that on this side of heaven, sin is with us to stay. No human has escaped that reality yet. And then broaden your gaze to see God at work. God has been living with the reality of human sin since Adam and Eve chose to disobey him. In the midst of that reality, God is more powerful than you can imagine. His power is at work within you. That is something to praise God for!

Practice Practice this "radical acceptance" of acknowledging sin by writing a prayer in your journal in which you 1) confess the reality of your sin 2) acknowledge that God is at work within you and 3) praise God for his power!

Devotion 122

"The kingdom of heaven is like a mustard seed,
which a man took and planted in his field. Though
it is the smallest of all seeds, yet when it grows, it is
the largest of garden plants and becomes a tree, so
that the birds come and perch in its branches."

MATTHEW 13:31–32

It's the small things in your day that can make or break it. Sure, big bonuses come along as well, but most good things come in the form of small gestures (a smile), small achievements (an answered email), or simple treats (what's your favorite?).

These small things are like mustard seeds, the place that God has put his kingdom of heaven. When we nurture the small seeds, they turn into huge plants and even trees that birds can perch in.

Your brain tends to skip over the pleasant things (the "mustard seeds") of life in search of something to worry about, just by virtue of the way it is wired. If you want to be happy and receive God's kingdom, one important step is learning to notice what is pleasant and then stick with that pleasant emotion. Allowing yourself to experience positive moments and then stay connected to those emotions for a bit each day is one of the ways that you can rewire your brain for more regular experiences of happiness.

Practice At least once today, notice a pleasant moment and any pleasant emotion that comes along with it. See if you can keep your attention on the pleasantness for 30 seconds (both thoughts and feelings) before you move on to the next thing.

Devotion 123

Once, on being asked by the Pharisees when the kingdom of God would come, Jesus replied, "The coming of the kingdom of God is not something that can be observed, nor will people say, 'Here it is,' or 'There it is,' because the kingdom of God is in your midst."

LUKE 17:20–21

Kings generally like lots of attention paid to them and their kingdoms, so it's notable that God's approach to kingship is different. He says you can't even see his kingdom coming—it's not a dramatic future that we're waiting around for, hoping to be rescued by our hero on a white horse. Instead, it's something that is already "in your midst" (or some Bible translations say "within you").

If you want to connect with God, start close. Look for God's kingdom within yourself and the communities of which you are a part. What is God already up to here? Where do you see God? Your initial response may be "nowhere—nothing to see here." That's okay, stay close and pay attention, and the clues will emerge.

It might be at a youth group meeting or a relaxing moment with people you love. It might be in a color you enjoy, an opportunity to care for someone, or an activity that sparks joy. It might be in a shared moment at a dark time. Start close, and you will find God's kingdom alive and well, right here within you.

Practice Following the body scan guide on page 166, pay attention to what is close—God's kingdom at work, right here within you. When you are finished, jot down some observations in your journal.

Devotion 124

Jesus . . . got up from the meal, took off his outer clothing, and wrapped a towel around his waist. After that, he poured water into a basin and began to wash his disciples' feet, drying them with the towel that was wrapped around him.

JOHN 13:3–5

While on earth, Jesus dealt with the same types of physical inconveniences that you do. Given the time he chose to enter history, he probably dealt with a few more physical challenges, actually. One of those was dirty feet.

In Jesus' time, feet got really dirty every day due to time spent in sandals walking the dusty roads. So when Jesus offered to wash his disciples' feet, it was a necessary and pretty gross task. Jesus did this as a humble demonstration of love, and he asked us to act in the same way toward one another.

Jesus valued giving care and attention to feet because he knew what it was like to have a body with physical needs. Tuning into the physical sensations in our feet can actually be a great way to ground ourselves, get out of our thoughts, and stabilize our emotions. Whether you are washing your feet or simply noticing them, you can know you are following Jesus' example.

Practice Following the sensing guide on page 180–181, choose the sense of touch. Take time to experience sensation specifically on the bottoms of your feet—simply paying attention to what your feet feel like. When you are finished, write a prayer of gratitude in your journal for God's care of your feet.

Whoever dwells in the shelter of the Most High
will rest in the shadow of the Almighty.

PSALM 91:1

Imagine that you are walking through a cold rainstorm, buffeted by the wind. You're not sure of your path, and you're longing for a dry and warm place. It's getting dark. It seems like your journey will never end. You're losing hope.

And then a home appears. The door opens, light spills out, and you are beckoned in. The warmth envelops you as you step over the threshold into the dwelling. You are handed dry clothes. You settle into a comfortable seat by the fireplace and breathe a sigh of relief as you wrap your thawing hands around a warm drink. You are safe, you are sheltered, you are at rest at last.

God gives us shelter every day. There are buildings that shelter you from harsh weather, clothes that keep you warm and protected. There are people who farm so you can eat, people who teach so you can learn. These are all invitations from God to "dwell" in his shelter. No matter how stormy things get, take some time today to rest in what God has provided.

Practice Following the breathing space guide on page 176–177, give yourself a couple minutes of rest. Notice your breath and/or whatever is provided for you in this moment. What supports you and gives you comfort? When you are finished, write a brief list in your journal of the things that God has given you in this moment as shelter.

Devotion 126

When [the disciples] landed, they saw a fire of burning coals there with fish on it, and some bread. . . . Jesus said to them, "Come and have breakfast."

JOHN 21:9, 12

Have you ever eaten fish (or something else you love) roasted over a beach bonfire? It doesn't get much better than that. And gathering around a warm fire at dawn, after a long night of fishing, would only make it that much more amazing.

This is how Jesus said "hello" to his disciples on one of those rare post-resurrection encounters with them, not too long before he said "goodbye" and ascended to heaven. He cooked for them. That aromatic blend of roasting food, charcoal, and sea water—combined with the sound of waves, the light of sunrise, and the sound of their risen Savior's voice—was one of their last memories with him.

Have you ever paid close attention to the smells, sights, and sounds of cooking a meal? Next time you prepare food, notice the incredible chemistry that occurs when ingredients come together. Cooking is amazing, a miracle every time, and it's no wonder Jesus gathered his disciples around a fire to cook together as one of their last memories together in the flesh.

Practice Participate in cooking something today. Pay attention to the smells, sights, and sounds of cooking. Notice the miracles of colors, aromas, and shapes as the food transforms before your eyes. When you are finished, thank God for the miracle of cooking.

Devotion 127

Then Peter came to Jesus and asked, "Lord, how many times shall I forgive my brother or sister who sins against me? Up to seven times?" Jesus answered, "I tell you, not seven times, but seventy-seven times."

MATTHEW 18:21–22

Forgiveness is giving up your right for retribution toward someone who has hurt you. But it does not mean allowing someone to continue harming you—you will sometimes need to set boundaries or even end a relationship that is toxic. But even our healthiest relationships require us to forgive repeatedly because no one loves perfectly. Forgiveness helps soften our grip on bitterness so it doesn't keep wounding us long after the initial pain is inflicted.

It's tough to forgive, especially when the pain is deep. Jesus talks about forgiving "seventy-seven times." In Scripture, this number is a representation of an unending, indescribable amount. But it can also be taken literally. If you set out to forgive 77 times, chances are your heart will start to heal in the course of all that letting go. Whether or not it makes a difference for the other person, it will make a difference for your own heart.

Practice Following the lovingkindness/blessing guide on page 172–173, choose a person that has hurt you. Practice letting go of bitterness by extending prayers of blessing to them. If this brings up painful emotions, show yourself kindness along the way and consider talking with a trusted adult or counselor about next steps in your healing journey.

Devotion 128

Throwing his cloak aside, he jumped to his feet and came to Jesus. "What do you want me to do for you?" Jesus asked him. The blind man said, "Rabbi, I want to see." "Go," said Jesus, "your faith has healed you." Immediately he received his sight and followed Jesus along the road.

MARK 10:50–52

Are there things you believe you shouldn't want? Scripture shows us how God can use our wants to lead us to him. Bartimaeus was a man without eyesight who heard Jesus coming. As he called out for healing of his blindness, he was rebuked by the crowd. They didn't think he should be wanting anything from Jesus. But Jesus made a point of stopping and asking Bartimaeus what he wanted. And then he gave him what he wanted—eyesight—and he highlighted his faith.

What do you want? Think a little different than the superficial, passing desires. Think instead of your *heart's* longing—like if Jesus was walking by and he could do anything for you, what would you ask him for?

Then, listen to that longing. Expressing it to Jesus is part of what it means to have faith.

Practice Following the centering prayer guide on page 184–185, notice what your heart longs for as you sit in God's presence. When you are finished, write a brief request in your journal expressing to God what you really want, allowing it to be an expression of faith in a God who loves you.

Devotion 129

Those who belong to Christ Jesus have crucified the flesh with its passions and desires. Since we live by the Spirit, let us keep in step with the Spirit. Let us not become conceited, provoking and envying each other.

GALATIANS 5:24–26

When you feel angry, the emotional alarm system of your brain flares up and makes it harder to think rationally or see any perspective besides your own. This is brain science, and it applies to all of us. You might have had an experience before of saying something in the heat of your anger that you regret later, perhaps leading you to hurt someone else or feel foolish about your actions.

This is "the flesh" talked about in this verse—these flareups that are not helpful. Managing anger well is important (and tricky), and it always involves slowing ourselves down. Fortunately, God is here to help you be in step with his Spirit, to slow down long enough to respond in a way you can feel good about later.

Next time you're tempted to charge into a conflict full-speed, consider an alternative. Perhaps you want to count to ten, focus on listening fully, or take a walk before you speak. The Spirit will help slow you down to his pace when you ask for help controlling your anger.

Practice Following the body scan guide on page 166, be curious about what urges come up in your body. Notice the option to slow down before responding. You have choices when it comes to responding to those brain signals. When you are finished, jot down some observations in your journal.

Devotion 130

Keep on loving one another as brothers and sisters. Do not forget to show hospitality to strangers, for by so doing some people have shown hospitality to angels without knowing it.

HEBREWS 13:1–2

Have you ever been the new kid? Walking into a new school, youth group, or social gathering for the first time can be energizing or just plain terrifying. If you've been through it, you probably weren't sure whether or not you would find friends, and that's tough.

We all have a responsibility to show kindness toward people we don't know yet. Your hospitality to kids on the margins doesn't have to be big and fancy right away. It's actually the little signals of acceptance that make a really big difference. Start with a smile. If someone looks lost, help them find something. If someone is sitting alone, invite them to sit with you. If someone doesn't get the inside joke, explain it. Be curious and friendly. Share a little of your own story. Let them know that they matter.

The Bible says some people who have shown this type of kindness to strangers have ended up talking to angels without even knowing it. How cool is that?

Practice Practice paying attention to the people around you today, noticing if there is anyone that may feel new, unnoticed, or marginalized. See if it's possible to turn some simple, kind attention toward them to help them feel seen and cared for. Afterwards, say a prayer for connection and acceptance in their life as you move on with your day.

Devotion 131

"Naked I came from my mother's womb,/ and naked I will depart./ The Lord gave and the Lord has taken away;/ may the name of the Lord be praised."

JOB 1:21

When people refer to your birthday suit, they're reminding you that you came into the world with nothing—completely naked. And you'll leave the world with nothing as well.

In between that naked beginning and ending, you'll have a variety of fortunes. Good times and bad times, happiness and sadness, prosperity and poverty, acceptance and rejection. God teaches us to accept these constant fluctuations as part of life, and mindfulness is a tool for this type of acceptance. We can learn to watch the constant change of life (even our feelings!) with neutral curiosity, just like we might watch changing weather.

God's truth and love remain strong through all the changes, whether you like them or not. You can choose to connect with God in the midst of what is difficult, bringing your honest thoughts and feelings into God's presence through the changing weather of your human experience. Praising God will keep you grounded in what is deeper than your feelings.

 Practice Following the sitting practice guide on page 167, practice nonjudgmental observation of your changing thoughts and feelings. Practice curiosity while noticing that God is solid and present through all of the changes. When you are finished, jot down some observations in your journal.

Devotion 132

God saw all that he had made, and it was very good.

GENESIS 1:31

Before you know if something is good or bad, you have to pay attention and really *see* it. This is where God started at the beginning of creation, by seeing what he made.

It's tempting to jump to the judgment, the part where you say something is good or bad. That can work sometimes, but it can also backfire. If you judge too quickly, you are less likely to be wise in your judgment.

Practice being like God and start with really *seeing*. Try paying attention to a moment like God did at the beginning of creation, seeing all of it, and sit with your observations and experiences before you judge them. Notice colors, shapes, textures, smells, tastes, feelings on your skin, breath in your body, emotions passing through. Be with them directly as if you've never experienced them before. Don't rush the judgment. Be patient with the seeing.

Of course, we know the judgment that God came to about creation (about you!) after he saw. "Very good." Perhaps you'll find some goodness too as you practice seeing and experiencing what God has created.

Practice Following the sensing guide on page 180–181, use your sense of sight to be present to whatever is in your environment right now. (Or if the sense of sight is not available to you, choose a different sense.) When you are finished, jot down some observations in your journal.

Devotion 133

My heart is not proud, LORD,/ my eyes are not haughty;/ I do not concern myself with great matters/ or things too wonderful for me./ But I have calmed and quieted myself,/ I am like a weaned child with its mother;/ like a weaned child I am content./ Israel, put your hope in the LORD/ both now and forevermore.

PSALM 131:1–3

You're accomplished at a lot. Are you haughty about what you can do? You can know your God-given gifts and talents without pretending you're "all that." A better-than-thou attitude closes you off to learning new things and pushes people away. In contrast, humility lets you lower your guard, learn new things, and rest in God's care.

One way to stay humble even as you grow your gifts is to stay in touch with your inner child. Sound silly? It is kind of silly, and it's also what God prescribes. Jesus tells us to be more like little children, and David in this psalm describes himself as being like a toddler all snuggled up with his mother—a child no longer demanding to nurse but instead at peace with mom.

Children don't know a lot; there's a lot that teens and adults don't know either. God gives you permission to "not know" stuff, just like a child—to be at peace in his care, and to be ready for surprise and delight as you learn new things!

Practice Do something that you might associate with being a child—blow bubbles, do somersaults. See if it's possible to relax and smile as you tune into the activity. When you are finished, jot down some observations in your journal.

Devotion 134

Jesus asked, "Were not all ten cleansed?
Where are the other nine?

LUKE 17:17

Gratitude is good for us—psychologists know from research that it boosts happiness. Scripture teaches us to say "thanks" on a regular basis, both to God and to one another.

You can start by noticing the ways people are helping you out, whether it's doing dishes or providing housing or inviting you to do something fun. And notice the ways God is getting you through hard times while gifting you with happy moments. You don't have to feel warm and fuzzy about it, it's okay to just say thanks.

There are also ways to cultivate grateful feelings through mindfulness. Practice paying attention to the "gifts" you receive each day, like the light shimmering on the top of your drink, the sound of a bird in the tree, the face of a person talking with you, or the solidness of a chair you are sitting in. Really noticing gifts will make it more possible for feelings of gratitude to break through the other noise in your mind. It's like reaching out your hands to receive the gift—noticing is the first step in gratitude.

Practice Following the stretching guide on page 170–171, imagine raising your hands in gratitude to God as you stretch up. Notice the ability of your body to move in this way, and allow the corners of your mouth to lift into a slight smile in response to this ability. When you are finished, jot down some observations in your journal.

Devotion 135

Then the man and his wife heard the sound of the L<small>ORD</small> God as he was walking in the garden in the cool of the day.

G<small>ENESIS</small> 3:8

People meet God in different ways and different places—some in church, others in private prayer or Scripture reading, others while walking in nature, others through music. Early in creation, Adam and Eve met God outside in a garden. God showed up taking an evening walk, and they were there too.

We don't know why God chose the "cool of the day" as the time for his walk, and it's interesting that the word cool here can also be translated as wind or breeze or storm. Even with the difficulty of translating this word, we see that Scripture is highlighting something here about the air in that moment. It's moving, it's cool, it's breezy. God was present in this breezy space, choosing to be in his creation and with his created people (even knowing they had just sinned).

Have you ever heard God outside while feeling the cool breeze on your skin? Tuning into the movement of air can alert us to God's presence. When you are outside taking a walk in the cool of the day, you can be sure that God will be there walking too. Don't forget to listen up for him.

> *Practice* While walking outside (whether it's a long walk in the woods or a short walk inside from the car), notice the air on your skin and notice that God is also out walking. Don't forget to listen for him and to say hello.

Devotion 136

*Let us draw near to God with a sincere heart and
with the full assurance that faith brings, having our
hearts sprinkled to cleanse us from a guilty conscience
and having our bodies washed with pure water.*

HEBREWS 10:22

Water is necessary for life. It keeps you hydrated and cleans your body. It's refreshing in swimming pools, calming in hot tubs, and life-giving for the plants and animals that feed you. It's used in baptism to symbolize salvation, blessing, and community. Water is a miracle.

When you feel guilty because of mistakes you have made, you may be tempted to hide in shame. Perhaps you don't want to tell anyone about your thoughts or actions because you feel dirty. But Jesus invites us to step out of hiding and come close because he has pure water to cleanse you—the miracle of forgiveness symbolized by the miracle of water.

Just like baptism with water, God is continuously cleansing our hearts. You can have full assurance that he is eager to meet you where you are. God is not looking for perfection, he is looking for sincerity. Come out of hiding and draw near to God, who is ready to wash you over and over with his love and forgiveness.

Practice Following the guide for centering prayer on page 184–185, draw near to God and stay in his presence. You can know that he is eager to meet you and always extend forgiveness. When you are finished, write a prayer in your journal receiving God's cleansing forgiveness.

Devotion 137

Whatever you do, work at it with all your heart, as working for the Lord, not for human masters.

COLOSSIANS 3:23

When you do an assignment or chore, do you give it all you've got? Do you beat yourself up when you don't think it's good enough, treating yourself poorly? Or maybe you do the bare minimum, hoping it's good enough without paying too much attention to quality? Would your work look different if you could see your loving God in front of you and knew you were doing it for him?

God says that all of your work should be wholehearted, as if you are doing the work for him. Whether your labors are for school, home, church, or a job, you are ultimately using your talents in service of God's kingdom. This doesn't mean working TOO hard—God is a gracious and loving employer! He wants you to work within your limits, doing your best without being overly harsh with yourself. But he knows that putting your whole heart in will bring you greater satisfaction in yourself and also maximize your contribution to his kingdom work in the world.

Practice Take a couple minutes to close your eyes (fully or partially) and imagine yourself doing a particular task—any type of work, study, or service you do on a regular basis. Imagine you are doing it for God who is with you, giving him your heart as you receive his love. When you are finished, write a brief prayer in your journal offering your work to him.

Devotion 138

He is before all things, and in him all things hold together.

COLOSSIANS 1:17

Ever feel like the world is unraveling? Between politics, natural disasters, and conflicts, it may sometimes seem that the entire planet is at war with itself. You may even feel at war with yourself sometimes, not sure of what you believe or who you are.

Christ offers something we desperately need when things are unraveling. He holds everything together. Human sin keeps things falling apart, like a sweater that keeps getting snagged. Jesus lovingly works those unraveling pieces back in so the whole thing holds together. He can do this because he has been here, from the beginning. Generation to generation, he has born witness to our human tendency to unravel as he carefully holds us together.

What divisions can you help to mend? When you find yourself drawn to make war with others or with yourself, consider that Jesus is before all things and that his final prayer before death was devoted to unity. He longs for his church to participate in holding all things together in love, more than battling over who is right.

Practice Following a sitting practice guide on page 167, notice any tendency to push away unwanted thoughts, feelings, and physical sensations. Experiment with an acceptance of each experience as it is, knowing that Christ holds you (and the world) together as your experiences come and go. When you are finished, jot down some observations in your journal.

Devotion 139

David and all the Israelites were celebrating with all their might before God, with songs and with harps, lyres, timbrels, cymbals and trumpets.

1 CHRONICLES 13:8

Sometimes we forget to notice and celebrate when we've reached our goals or when God has provided for our needs. It's easier to just jump into the next worry, the next desperate prayer, the next goal. It's possible to get through all of life without ever really pausing to celebrate what has been received and achieved.

King David modeled celebration for us. He noticed when God showed up for him and he often responded with a party.

You'll have big achievements that call for pulling out all the stops like King David, like when you graduate or get your first job. And then you'll have small achievements that call for a quiet little party inside your heart, like when you stick with a hard homework assignment and tell yourself "Good job" with a smile.

Learning to notice and celebrate the good is one of the ways you can cultivate happiness and gratitude in your life.

Practice Take a couple minutes to close your eyes (fully or partially) and identify one thing you have accomplished in the past 24 hours, even if it's just getting out of bed. Notice any resistance to recognizing your accomplishment, then smile at yourself and say "Good job" as you thank God for his provision. When you are finished, write a brief note in your journal celebrating what God has helped you to do.

Devotion 140

Godliness with contentment is great gain. For we brought nothing into the world, and we can take nothing out of it. But if we have food and clothing, we will be content with that.

1 Timothy 6:6–8

Contentment can be hard to come by in a world that says you always need to buy more, do more, and be more. Scripture reveals a simpler way to live, focused on what you have instead of what you don't have. When your mind is not consumed with having more, you have more room to notice God and to be transformed by his spirit.

One way to practice contentment is to pay more attention to what has been provided for you. In this verse, you are encouraged to notice that you have food and clothing. There is nothing in the Scripture about what type of food and clothing, you are just encouraged to be content with the food and clothing that you have.

This type of acceptance is challenging and also freeing. God is giving you permission to say "Good enough" and to enjoy your life as it is. You'll still want to grow and change, to advocate for kingdom transformation in the world when it comes to the things that really matter. But if you have food in your belly and clothes on your body, you are invited to see that you are provided for—life is good.

 Practice Following the sensing meditation guide on page 180–181, choose the touch of clothing as the focus of your attention. Notice sensations where your clothing touches your skin—textures, pressure, temperature. When you are finished, jot down some observations in your journal.

Devotion 141

He has made everything beautiful in its time. He has also set eternity in the human heart; yet no one can fathom what God has done from beginning to end.

ECCLESIASTES 3:11

You have probably worked to make something beautiful or attractive—your room, an outfit, your hair in the morning, a piece of artwork. Making things look nice is part of how we reflect God's image, because God also makes things beautiful. If you've seen a picture of the earth from space or taken time to look into the eyes of someone you love, you know that God's creation is beautiful.

The things we create are beautiful, but not in the same way that our eternal God is creating beauty in the universe. Your creative work is like a child's drawing that is loved and admired by a parent but perhaps not on par with the masterpieces hanging in the world's greatest art museums. God loves our artwork and he loves us. Our creative work brings joy to his heart. He also has a much more comprehensive, much more eternal type of creativity at work.

Just like a child with their parent, we can't even fathom the whole beautiful picture of what God is creating over time. But we do get to be part of this eternal work of beauty. That's awesome!

Practice Take a few minutes to draw or color, keeping it simple. Pay attention to the colors, shapes, textures of what you put on paper—tune into the beauty without overthinking it. Consider that this small piece of colorful beauty is part of God's grand beautiful design over time.

Devotion 142

You are all children of the light and children of the day. We do not belong to the night or to the darkness. So then, let us not be like others, who are asleep, but let us be awake and sober.

1 Thessalonians 5:5–6

The fancier our technology gets, the easier it gets to move through the day numbed and thoughtless. For example, you might feel uncomfortable with your thoughts so you pull out your phone and start scrolling social media. You might feel anxious in a social situation so you get in the car and drive away. You might feel angry about a life circumstance so you fire off thoughtless words online.

Living "awake and sober" means choosing awareness over numbness. This can be uncomfortable, as it involves feeling the things and having the conversations. It involves taking care of your anxiety, anger, or sadness instead of ignoring it. It involves slow, thoughtful responses instead of hot takes. It involves getting off the screen and actually sitting with people (and yourself).

Why go through this kind of discomfort? Because living life with eyes wide open also brings joy! When we let ourselves feel things and be with people, we become awake enough to enjoy the things that God has given us.

Practice Following the stretching/yoga guide on page 170–171, use the movement of your body to be "awake" to the moment. Tune into your physical experience as you move as a way of increasing awareness. When you are finished, jot down some observations in your journal.

Devotion 143

'Love your neighbor as yourself.'

MARK 12:31

Jesus wasn't known for quick tips or easy fixes, and his command to love your neighbor is no exception. This is hard stuff.

Have you ever had a neighbor who interrupted your sleep or safety? A classmate who said rude things or smelled bad? A person living nearby on the streets who asked for money? Or maybe a global neighbor who threatened your country in some way?

While some neighbors are easy to love (hooray for the lady next door who bakes you cookies!), you'll have lots of nearby people in your life who are hard to love. Jesus tells you to love them anyway.

How that plays out will look a little different in each situation and for each person. Some neighbor relationships will be best if you build a fence or pray blessings from a distance. But Jesus is quite clear that loving your neighbor is not optional. You are required to consider the wellbeing of your neighbor. Do not harm them as if they were worth less than you, do not ignore them as if they were inhuman, do not simplify them as if they were caricatures of evil. Love your neighbor in the same way you love yourself.

Practice Following the lovingkindness/blessing guide on page 172–173, practice extending love to a neighbor of your choosing, as well as to yourself. When you are finished, jot down some observations in your journal.

Devotion 144

Those who hope in the LORD/ will renew their strength./
They will soar on wings like eagles;/ they will run and
not grow weary,/ they will walk and not be faint.

ISAIAH 40:31

The stress and strain of life can be pretty intense at times. Like a marathon runner, you have to plan for how to sustain your strength over the long haul. If you think "normal" people shouldn't have to practice self-care to keep their strength up, think again—we all have to implement intentional practices to take care of ourselves through life's rough patches, just like a marathon runner has to train and fuel in very particular ways if they're going to finish the race.

Fortunately, God's got your back. Keeping your hope in him is step one to having what you need. You can't push through life on your own and expect it to go well. God wants to refresh and renew you. On your own, you will get weary and faint. But God will give you the boost you need when your strength starts to flag. Practices like prayer and meditation, along with God's gifts of exercise, creativity, social connection, and nutritious eating, are examples of practices that can help you stay rooted in God's sustaining strength. With your hope in God, you will be renewed to stay in the race.

Practice Following the walking/wheeling guide on page 168–169, use this time of movement to notice the strength God provides for you along the way, each muscle renewed by him for its task. When you are finished, jot down some observations in your journal.

"The LORD is my strength and my defense;/ he has become my salvation./ He is my God, and I will praise him,/ my father's God, and I will exalt him.

EXODUS 15:2

The fight-flight-freeze response helps keep you safe from danger. It can help you quickly and instinctively defend yourself, escape, or hide out until a threat passes.

But sometimes this response becomes unhelpful. For example, you might find yourself picking a fight with someone because of a perceived putdown (fight response), or bolting from a social situation because of a fear of judgment (flight response), or staying glued to your phone when someone is trying to have a difficult conversation with you (freeze response). Your fight-flight-freeze response in these situations is like an overactive alarm, more likely to cause problems.

This is just one of the ways that God's ways are higher than yours—his alarm system is more sophisticated. He is your strength and salvation. While your fight-flight-freeze response can help out, your wellbeing ultimately depends on him.

When you find your protective impulses to be overactive, you can take a breath and know that God is defending you.

Practice Following the working with difficulty guide on page 178–179, notice any fight-flight-freeze response to your difficulty. While your body and mind react, know that God is your strength and defender. When you are finished, write a prayer surrendering your difficulty to God.

Devotion 146

"The virgin will conceive and give birth to a son, and they will call him Immanuel" (which means "God with us").

MATTHEW 1:23

When Jesus came to earth, there was no such thing as incarnation yet. God had been inaccessible, and his words had to be brought by religious professionals. So this move of coming to earth as both Son of Man and of God was a big deal, and it changed our access to God.

The name Immanuel sums it all up, meaning God With Us, and Jesus' time on earth was followed by the coming of the Holy Spirit to be with us forever. We now live in a world where God is nearby, and we don't just hear about him from the professionals. We get to talk to him ourselves and experience him directly.

This has huge implications for mindfulness practice. It means that when we slow ourselves down to pay attention to the present moment, we have the capacity to perceive God right here with us. Our nonjudgmental, accepting, curious observation of the moment through mindfulness meditation can lead us to observe God at work and the gifts God has given.

When you practice mindfulness with an awareness of God With Us, you have the capacity to strengthen your spiritual walk at the same time that you care for your mental health.

Practice Following the breathing space guide on page 176–177, practice noticing the present moment along with God's presence here with you. When you are finished, jot down some observations in your journal.

Devotion 147

Where can I go from your Spirit?
Where can I flee from your presence?

PSALM 139:7

You can never get away from God. Plenty of people have tried to separate themselves from God by ignoring him, disproving him, or literally running away from him (maybe you've heard about Jonah's little incident with the whale when he tried that?). But it's just a fact that no matter how we feel about it, God is with us all the time.

Mindfulness practice involves accepting whatever is present without judgment. When you practice this kind of radical acceptance, one of the things you can practice is noticing God's presence. God stays with you all the time because he loves you and he wants to be with you. Your purpose in life is to be in relationship with God. Also, God is the sustainer of your life in every moment, so you need God to survive.

You don't have to feel any special way about God being here—sometimes it might feel a bit too vulnerable, and that's okay. But know that he loves you, he sustains you, and opening up to his presence over time is a pathway to greater joy, peace, and contentment in your life.

Practice Following the walking/wheeling meditation on page 168–169, notice that God stays present with you as you move your feet or wheel your chair through space. When you are finished, jot down some observations in your journal.

Devotion 148

Give thanks in all circumstances; for this is
God's will for you in Christ Jesus.
1 THESSALONIANS 5:18

You may say thank you pretty easily if someone were to make your favorite dessert or hand you a million dollars. But what about when you are struggling with difficult circumstances, like a loss or a big regret?

God asks us to be grateful in all circumstances, even if you don't feel like it. He is working good out of every situation—good that you may not see until much later. You might think of this like a surgeon who causes pain and discomfort in order to save your life. At the time, it may be hard to accept the "goodness" of the pain inflicted, even if you know it's for your good in the long run.

At the same time, don't be afraid to feel what you feel. Tears are often helpful in healing, and expressing yourself authentically will keep you emotionally healthy. Lament is a part of what is modeled for us in Scripture, and you get to be honest about the hard times just like the authors of Scripture (and just like God). But you can know that whatever you feel, God is good all the time.

Practice Following the working with difficulty guide on page 178–179, see if you can notice your thoughts and feelings about a challenging circumstance. Invite God to do the work of a surgeon in this circumstance, knowing that the pain is part of your healing journey. When you are finished, jot down some observations in your journal.

*At sunset, the people brought to Jesus all who
had various kinds of sickness, and laying his
hands on each one, he healed them.*

LUKE 4:40

Healing flowed through Jesus' hands and fingers. When he healed people, he often touched them. What could that have felt like to him? Were there physical sensations involved as power flowed through his fingers? What kind of care did he give his hands, day in and day out, in preparation for them to conduct healing power?

Like Jesus, you also have hands that can convey care, warmth, safe touch, and assistance for others. Or they can convey aggression, power, unsafe touch, and disregard for others' dignity. You will want to use your hands wisely in life. Notice how they are being used. Notice what kind of reaction you get from others when you use them.

So much of healing presence for others involves paying attention to their needs and your resources. Don't forget to pay attention to this resource of your hands. As you tune into the physical sensations in your hands and fingers, you may be surprised at how much healing can be conveyed through a simple touch.

Practice Following the sensing meditation guide on page 180–181, focus your attention on the tips of your fingers. Notice sensations for a couple minutes—temperature, blood flow, pulsing, contact, or any other sensations that come. When you are finished, jot down some observations in your journal.

Devotion 150

As they make music they will sing "All my fountains are in you."

PSALM 87:7

You may be carrying the weight of the world on your shoulders. You may be trying to pull yourself up by your own bootstraps. Maybe you're pushing ahead, clambering to the top, trying to prove yourself to the world. It's tough being alone.

Living only out of your own strength will leave you crushed in the end. You are not made to function alone—God has provided a source of strength to sustain you. His very presence is an eternal fountain from which you can draw everything you need.

Mindfulness is one way to notice your useless striving and pushing, giving you the option to stop clambering up (possibly knocking others down as you climb) and start reaching down into the fountains of provision that God provides. Those fountains can get buried deep over time if we're not paying attention, so don't be afraid to slow down and take all the time you need to dig deep for God's fountains of provision. That cool, clean water will feel so refreshing to your soul once you have tapped down into it.

Practice Following the sitting guide on page 167, take a few minutes of silence to notice any anxious striving in your mind and to allow your attention to settle with your breath. Be aware that there is a fountain of provision deep within you, put there by God. When you are finished, jot down some observations in your journal.

Mindfulness Meditation Guides

The devotionals throughout this book are accompanied by mindfulness practices for you to use in connecting with God in the present moment. While some of these are *informal* mindfulness practices that can be used any time during the day, there are also several *formal* mindfulness practices that invite you to set aside a few minutes of intentional time.

The following *formal* mindfulness practices match up with symbols that you'll see throughout this devotional collection. Each is written to be used for as little as 3 minutes, with the option of longer practices as well—10-20 minutes is a common length of time for mindfulness meditation. If you work best with some outside direction during meditation (as many of us do), you can choose instead to listen to the audio guides for Christian mindfulness meditation at www.TheMindfulChristian.com.

Here are some tips for getting the most out of your formal mindfulness practice:

- Find a quiet place where you do not expect to be interrupted.
- Have a blanket on hand in case you feel chilly—body temperature tends to drop during meditation.
- Set a timer before you start so you aren't watching the clock during your meditation.

- Modify the postures and the instructions in any way that works best for your mind and body—you are the expert on your own experience.

One common mistake in meditation is to think you have to feel a certain way (like calm) or have a certain experience (like peaceful thoughts) to benefit. The goal of mindfulness meditation is just to notice whatever is in the moment, even if it's uncomfortable. So don't feel you need to change anything as you meditate or do it any differently. You're just becoming aware and letting God do the rest.

If you are experiencing any difficulties related to physical or mental health, you are encouraged to consult with a professional before embarking on these meditations—a doctor or therapist can be helpful in adapting the practices to your particular needs. This is especially important if you have any history of trauma (physical or mental), suicidal thoughts, substance misuse, or psychosis.

If you ever feel overwhelmed during a meditation, give yourself permission to stop the meditation or to change it in a way that feels more comfortable for you. For example, you might choose to open your eyes, focus on a "safe" sensation in your body, or listen to sounds around you. God is with you, and you have the choice to move your attention to whatever feels safe and anchoring in the moment. Whatever your experience, consider talking with an adult that you trust about your experiences with Christian mindfulness meditation in order to maximize your benefit.

Body Scan

This meditation practice invites you to move attention through your body in order to become aware of physical sensations. In the process, you are likely to also notice thoughts, feelings, behaviors/urges, and God's presence. This is a way to become more acquainted with your body as a wonderful creation of God!

1. Lie on your back on a firm surface with feet apart, toes falling away from one another, and arms at your sides.
2. Get comfortable. Close your eyes if you choose, or close them halfway with a soft gaze.
3. Take a couple deep breaths, then allow your breathing to return to its normal rate. Notice the sensations of your breath coming in and out.
4. Move your attention down to your toes. Notice what you feel there—maybe temperature, contact, tingling, etc.
5. Gradually move your attention through your body, pausing to notice what you feel in each body part. Move slowly from your toes all the way up to the top of your head.
6. As you pay attention to your body, see if you can notice your physical sensations directly, without overthinking them or trying to change anything. Be curious, not judgmental.
7. When you are done, notice the feeling of your whole body lying here, held together by your skin. Thank God for this wonderful creation of your body and continue on to your next activity.

Sitting Practice

The instructions for this meditation practice are how most people think of meditating—sitting with a straight back, closing your eyes, and focusing your mind. The primary focus will be your breath, but you may choose to "anchor" your attention anywhere you would like as you go through the practice (ex. sounds around you).

1. Sit at the edge of a chair with your feet on the floor (or cross-legged on a meditation cushion) with a straight spine and hands on your thighs or lap.

2. Get comfortable. Close your eyes if you choose, or close them halfway with a soft gaze.

3. Take a couple deep breaths, then allow your breathing to return to its normal rate. Notice the sensations of your breath coming in and out.

4. Choose where to "anchor" your attention—you can remain focused on your breath coming in and out, or choose somewhere else to focus.

5. As you pay attention to your breathing (or other anchor), see if you can experience it directly rather than thinking about it or trying to change it. Be curious, not judgmental.

6. When you are done, take a deep breath and open up your attention to the space around you. Thank God for the breath you are receiving in your body and continue on to your next activity.

Walking/Wheeling Meditation

This practice will help you become more aware of the miracle of walking or moving a wheelchair—all the many movements and sensations involved in moving our bodies through space. We often walk or wheel along with our minds in a completely different place than where we are, lost in stories and interpretations that have nothing to do with the moment. This meditation (involving very slow movement) shifts your attention from your head down into your body so you can be aware of your moment-to-moment experience as you journey.

1. Stand still—or if you are using a wheelchair, sit still—for a moment. If you choose, close your eyes halfway with a soft gaze. Take a couple deep breaths, then allow your breathing to return to its normal rate.

2. Feel your feet and/or body grounded in the surface beneath you. Notice the firmness of the earth holding you up.

3. For a walking meditation, begin to walk, focusing your attention on the sensations of your feet and legs moving through the air. See if you can notice each part of each step—the heel lifting, the ball of the foot lifting, the toes coming off the ground, the body shifting weight, the foot and leg moving through space, the heel reconnecting with the earth.

   For a wheeling meditation, begin to roll your chair, focusing on the specific sensations involved in moving. For example, you might feel your hand cradling the joystick or connecting with the wheel, your muscles yielding to the seat, and your body responding to the various textures and surfaces that you wheel over.

4. As you pay attention to the physical sensations of walking/wheeling, see if you can experience them directly rather than thinking about them or trying to change them. Each time you notice that you're back in thinking mode, return your attention to a direct awareness of your body moving through space.

5. Experiment with walking/wheeling at different speeds, seeing if your attention is more focused when you move more slowly. Some people practice this at such a slow pace that you can hardly see them moving.

6. When you are done, take a deep breath and open up your attention to the space around you. Thank God for the miracle of walking/wheeling and continue on to your next activity.

Stretching/Yoga Meditation

Your mind and body are constantly interacting with one another, and this stretching practice will utilize some simple yoga poses to increase your awareness of that interaction. It will also help you loosen up some tense muscles.

1. Stand still (or sit still) for a moment, with your arms at your sides. If you choose, close your eyes halfway with a soft gaze. Take a couple deep breaths, then allow your breathing to return to its normal rate. Notice that God is with you.

2. Feel your feet and/or body grounded in the surface beneath you. Notice the firmness of the earth holding you up.

3. Turn a kind attention toward your body, releasing any harsh or self-critical tone that might creep into your thoughts. Any time during this practice that you notice judgments, you might smile at yourself and gently move your attention back into your body.

4. If it is accessible to you, take a deep breath in and slowly lift your arms up so they are above your head. Keeping your shoulders soft, stretch your hands up while rooting down firmly with your feet or body. As you breathe out, lower your arms down again.

5. Now on an in-breath lift one arm up slowly, following your hand with your eyes as it moves. Stretch up with that hand, as if you are reaching to pick a piece of fruit from a tree above. When you are ready, on an out-breath, bring that hand down slowly (drinking in colors and shapes as your eyes follow it down), and then repeat on the other side.

6. On an in-breath, move both arms up above your head. On an out-breath, bring your arms down toward the floor as you allow your entire upper body to bend down, dangling from the waist as far as your body goes. Adapt this to your particular needs and abilities, noticing with gratitude what your body is able to do. Continue to breathe.

7. When you are ready, roll up slowly through your back, one vertebra at a time. Take a deep breath in as you raise your arms toward the ceiling and look up, lowering your arms and eyes down again on the out-breath.

8. You can repeat these simple stretches as many times as you would like, along with any others that feel good to your muscles (notice what your body is asking for).

9. When you are done, take a deep breath and open up your attention to the space around you. Thank God for the miracle of movement and continue on to your next activity.

Lovingkindness/Blessing Practice

Being kind toward ourselves and others can take some practice, and this meditation is a chance to practice that kind of compassion in our thoughts. It can be used as a prayer or blessing—lifting ourselves and others before God as we hope for good things.

1. Identify one or more people to whom you will practice extending lovingkindness, choosing from the following categories:

   Yourself

   Someone you love, care about, or admire, who brings you warm feelings when you think about them

   Someone you do not know well, a stranger or distant acquaintance

   Someone who is difficult for you, who you do not get along with well or who has caused you some pain

   All people, animals, and plants in the world, all living beings everywhere

2. Sit at the edge of a chair with your feet on the floor (or cross-legged on a meditation cushion) with a straight spine and hands on your thighs or lap. Alternately, you may choose to lie on your back on a firm surface with feet apart, toes falling away from one another, and arms at your sides.

3. Get comfortable. Close your eyes if you choose, or close them halfway with a soft gaze.

4. Take a couple deep breaths, then allow your breathing to return to its normal rate. Notice the sensations of your breath coming in and out.

5. One at a time, bring to mind an image of yourself or the person(s) to whom you are extending compassion. If you would like, you can imagine them resting in God's loving hands. Recognize that like everyone, you and/or the other person in your mind is in need of compassion.

6. With each image in mind, choose one of these two sets of phrases (or a different set of compassionate phrases that is more comfortable for you) and repeat them several times toward each of the people you have chosen to extend compassion to during your practice. As you repeat the phrases, recognize that all people desire these good things, and all people are loved by God.

7. When you are done, rest for a moment in the compassionate kindness you have practiced. Then take a deep breath and open up your attention to the space around you. Thank God for his lovingkindness toward us all and continue on to your next activity.

Mountain Meditation

The Bible is rich with imagery and metaphors that illuminate our understanding of ourselves and God. This meditation uses the imagery of a mountain to help ground you in the stability God has created within you—the strength that sustains you in the midst of life's constant changes.

1. Sit at the edge of a chair with your feet on the floor (or cross-legged on a meditation cushion) with a straight spine and hands on your thighs or lap. Alternatively, stand up straight with your feet firmly rooted in the floor and the top of your head reaching up toward the sky—allow your arms to hang loosely at your sides and make sure your knees remain unlocked throughout the practice.

2. Get comfortable. Close your eyes if you choose, or close them halfway with a soft gaze.

3. Take a couple deep breaths, then allow your breathing to return to its normal rate. Notice the sensations of your breath coming in and out.

4. Expand your awareness to the feeling of breath moving through your whole body, and notice your body sitting/standing here as a cohesive whole.

5. Imagine that you are a mountain. The weight of gravity holds you down, heavy and connected to the earth. The top of your head is a peak, reaching up with pride and dignity to the sky.

6. Imagine the many things living on the mountain (trees, plants, and animals) and imagine the movement of water across the mountain's surface (rivers, waterfalls, and lakes).

7. Imagine changing weather patterns moving across the mountain—calm days (with sun and mild temperatures), thunderstorms (with thunder and lightning), blizzards (burying everything in snow), hot days, cold days.

8. Notice and acknowledge your stability and groundedness through all of the changes.

9. When you are done, take a deep breath and open up your attention to the space around you. Thank God that you are created strong and resilient, ready for what each moment brings, grounded in divine providence and provision. Then continue on to your next activity.

Breathing Space

This practice is similar to a regular sitting practice, but it is meant to be more portable—an opportunity to quickly "drop in" at any point during the day to check in with how you are doing. The practice is often divided into three one-minute sections that have an hourglass shape of awareness (see below). However, there is no need to time each minute separately; just set your timer for three minutes if you choose, and then estimate one minute for each of the three sections.

1. Pause wherever you are and become still. If you're able, close your eyes if you choose, or close them halfway with a soft gaze. Take a couple deep breaths, then allow your breathing to return to its normal rate. Recognize that you are in God's presence.

2. First minute: Starting with a broad awareness, check in with what is going on for you in the moment. This "wide awareness" is the top part of the hourglass shape in this meditation. You might notice things in these different areas:

   Physical sensations, including your breath moving in and out

   Thoughts going through your mind

   Emotions, either prominent or under the surface

   Behaviors or urges you are having

3. Second minute: Narrowing your attention to breathing (as the middle part of the hourglass shape), notice where you feel your breath most vividly (ex. your upper lip, shoulders

moving, chest expanding/contracting, belly moving up and down). Rest your attention there, paying close attention to the sensations of your breath coming in and out of your body, given by God. If focusing on breath is triggering for you, choose a different anchor for your attention that allows you to regulate your emotions more effectively.

4. Third minute: Broadening your attention once again (as the bottom "wide awareness" part of the hourglass shape), imagine that your whole body is breathing. Imagine the air moving all the way from your head down to your toes, and then back out through your body again. Allow your whole body to experience the breath of life, given by God, restoring your body and soul, one moment at a time.

5. When you are done, open up your attention to the space around you. Notice if there are any adjustments needed in your circumstances or self-care in response to what you noticed during the practice. Thank God for this moment of life and continue on to your next activity!

This practice is an opportunity to pay special attention to any challenges that you are experiencing, noticing a tendency to ignore or avoid the difficulties and instead staying with them for purposes of opening up to God's healing.

1. Sit at the edge of a chair with your feet on the floor (or cross-legged on a meditation cushion) with a straight spine and hands on your thighs or lap. Alternately, you may choose to lie on your back on a firm surface with feet apart, toes falling away from one another, and arms at your sides.

2. Get comfortable. Close your eyes if you choose, or close them halfway with a soft gaze.

3. Take a couple deep breaths, then allow your breathing to return to its normal rate. Notice the sensations of your breath coming in and out.

4. Become aware of a difficulty that is present in your life right now—not your most difficult challenge, but something in the mild to moderate range. See if you can allow your attention to rest with that difficulty for a bit.

5. Notice what comes along with that difficulty, aware of the following areas:

    Physical sensations, including your breath moving in and out

    Thoughts going through your mind

    Emotions, either prominent or under the surface

    Behaviors or urges you are having

6. See if you can keep observing the difficulty without judgment or analysis, just continuing to notice what comes along with it. As much as possible, keep an attitude of compassion and kindness toward yourself.

7. Allow yourself to rest in God's presence as you stay present to your difficulty, without needing anything to be changed or different. Feel whatever you need to feel. Know that you are in God's hands.

8. When you are done, open up your attention to the space around you. Thank God for being with you through life's challenges, and see if you can bring an attitude of self-compassion with you as you continue on to your next activity.

Sensing Meditation

Our body is bringing in so much information through our senses all the time that we miss most of it! This meditation helps open you up to what your body is experiencing, awakening you to God's miraculous creation revealed through your senses. Once you've followed the sensing meditation in a formal sense, you might want to try just increasing your awareness through the day of sensory input.

1. Identify one sense that you will focus on, choosing from the following categories:

   > Hearing—sounds near or far
   > Seeing—shapes, colors, light/dark, patterns
   > Touching—textures, contours, pressure
   > Smelling—aromas
   > Tasting—food, drink, or any taste in mouth

2. Get comfortable in a seated position.

3. Tune into whichever sense you've chosen. Rather than searching for sensory input (sounds, sights, textures, smells, and tastes), simply allow the sensory input to come to you and then pass away all in its own time.

4. See if it is possible to observe the sensory input directly rather than through the filter of language, noticing what the experience is like just before your mind has put a label on it.

5. Whenever you notice that your mind has wandered away from sensory input, smile at yourself and bring your attention back to where you intended it to be.

6. When you are done, take a deep breath and open up your attention to the space around you. Thank God for the wealth of sensory input available to you in each moment and continue on to your next activity.

Eating Meditation

Food is our fuel, and we literally need it for everything we do. Also, it can be fun and delicious! This meditation helps us tune into the experience of eating as well as the way that our food connects us with God and the rest of the world. As you eat, notice God's presence with you and the way that this food is nourishing your body.

1. Find something to eat, preferably something simple and unprocessed like a raisin or other fruit. Sit in a quiet place and prepare to bring your full focus to the food with curiosity, as if you have just dropped in from another planet and have never seen this object before.

2. Hold the food in your hand and notice how it looks, including color, shape, symmetry, darkness, patterns, etc.

3. Consider the journey this food has been on. (If your food contains multiple ingredients, you might consider choosing just one in order to avoid getting overwhelmed!) For example, God may have used many people to get this food to you, including farmers, truck drivers, grocery store workers, and parents/guardians. It is likely that there was sun and rain that touched the food as it grew, and technology systems that enabled people to grow, nurture, harvest, and transport the food. Notice how this food demonstrates our deep interconnectedness with each other, the earth, and God.

4. Notice thoughts you are experiencing, without judging them

(even if they're thoughts like "This is a dumb meditation!"), and then bring your attention back to the food in your hand.

5. Hold the food close to your ear and move it around a bit, noticing if it makes any sounds as it is manipulated.

6. Allow yourself to drink in the smell of the food, and observe any reactions in your mouth, stomach, thoughts, or feelings in response to smelling.

7. When you put the food in your mouth for chewing, take your time. Notice how your body knows how to get it into your mouth and what to do once it is there. Observe the changes of texture and taste as you chew, and observe the movement of the food down into your stomach.

8. When you are done, take a deep breath and open up your attention to the space around you. Thank God for providing you with food to eat that helps keep your body, mind, and emotions as strong as they can, and then continue on to your next activity.

Centering Prayer

This prayer practice is not a traditional mindfulness practice, but it can easily be converted into a mindfulness practice for Christians. Through centering prayer, you will be focusing on God's presence as the object of your attention, just as you might focus in other mindfulness practices on different parts of the present moment (such as physical sensations or emotions).

1. As you prepare to "anchor" your attention in God, choose a prompt that you will use during the practice to remind you of God's presence. This could either be your breath or a word (such as peace or love or Father).

2. Find a comfortable seated position, perhaps with your back straight and your feet on the floor. Close your eyes if you choose, or close them halfway with a soft gaze.

3. Take a couple deep breaths, then allow your breathing to return to its normal rate. Notice the sensations of your breath coming in and out.

4. Settle your attention on the near presence of God, within you or in the room. No need to think about God, see if you can just notice that you and God are together.

5. Allow each breath to serve as a reminder of God's presence—or if you've chosen a word as your prompt, allow that word to be repeated quietly and lightly in the back of your mind as a way to connect you with God. Each time you notice your mind has wandered away, smile and gently bring your attention back to God's presence with you in the moment.

6. When you are done, take a deep breath and open up your attention to the space around you. Thank God for his divine presence that is with you all the time and continue on to your next activity!

FAQs:
The Nuts and Bolts of Meditation

1. *Is mindfulness Buddhist, and is it okay*
   for Christians to practice it?

   People from every major world religion have been practicing meditation throughout human history because paying attention is crucial for finding God (and silence is a great way to practice paying attention). Having said that, mindfulness is one type of meditation that is often practiced from a secular approach without any religious connection. While some mindfulness practitioners choose to apply a Buddhist framework, mindfulness can just as easily be blended with Christian faith, with a different faith, or with no faith at all.

   You can think of this like prayer, forgiveness, or even practices of physical health like exercise and hygiene—the fact that people of other faiths practice them does not take away from the power of practicing them as a Christian. Jesus invites us to pay attention to his kingdom work in the world, and mindfulness meditation is a wonderful way to do that!

2. *How do I get better at meditation? My mind wanders*
   all over the place and it's really hard to sit still.

   There is a misconception that meditation leads us to feel

calm and relaxed, and that you are "not good at meditation" if you do not experience a focused and clear mind during practice. In reality, most meditators find their mind wandering and their body fidgeting quite a bit. This is an expected part of the experience, and mindfulness is a chance to observe that movement in your mind and body without judging it as good or bad or forcing it to be different.

In other words, you can't fail at meditation. As you practice more, you'll find it easier to observe your thoughts and feelings without judgment, and you will experience calm and relaxed feelings during your practice at times. But this won't come from forcing it. Allow mindfulness meditation to be a chance to give up the need to perform well, and just be curious about whatever happens during your practice as God does his work in your life.

3. *What if my body gets really uncomfortable when I meditate?*

You will definitely get uncomfortable while you meditate, just like you do in the rest of your life at times. The goal of mindfulness meditation is to be "skillful" in how you respond to that discomfort. This means you slow down your response and pay attention to whether or not that response is helpful. (A lot of the ways we deal with our physical discomfort don't actually help, but we keep doing them anyway, like ignoring tense muscles or fidgeting incessantly.) This will help you be more intentional in the rest of your life too.

Some things you can try when you're physically uncomfortable are:

- Notice your physical sensation—the shape, size, and specific sensation. Notice if it is changing in any way moment to moment.
- Breathe right into the area of discomfort, imagining your breath flowing in and out of it.
- See if the sensation changes all on its own, without you moving. Notice any urges to move, and see what it's like not to obey those urges right away.
- If you choose to move, do it slowly and intentionally. Pay attention to the impact your movement has on the sensation.

4. *What if I feel more anxious while I meditate?*

You will feel anxious while you meditate, and probably a host of other feelings too like sadness, anger, and impatience. This is you getting in touch with yourself during the practice, and it's a good thing. Just like physical discomfort (see #3 above), the emotional discomfort will come and go during your practice as it does in the rest of your life.

Some things you can try when you're emotionally uncomfortable are:

- Notice your emotion. Notice if it is being triggered by any specific thoughts, and notice if your emotion is changing in any way moment to moment.
- See if you can give up the need for that emotion to change in order for you to be "okay"—in other words, is it possible to sit with this emotion as it is, trusting that you can tolerate it and it will pass?

- Give yourself permission to change the practice if anxiety (or another feeling) becomes too intense. You can change what you are focusing on as an act of self-compassion. For example, if focusing on your breath consistently triggers anxiety, you might choose a different "anchor" for your attention like the sensations on the bottom of your feet or a certain color in the room. Be aware of what you are doing with your mind as you are doing it.

Meditating can be a bit like pulling up a chair for your anxiety and other emotions, sitting with them for a while in a spirit of compassion toward yourself. God is with you as you do this healing (and sometimes uncomfortable!) work over time.

5. *Are there other kinds of meditation besides mindfulness?*

Yes! Mindfulness meditation is the practice of paying attention to the present moment with an accepting attitude of nonjudgmental, open curiosity. Other types of meditation might include focusing on written passages (like Scripture meditation), relaxing scenes in your imagination (like guided imagery), or repeating particular words (like a mantra).

All types of meditation include putting your focus on something in particular—so a meditation's compatibility with Christian faith is dependent on what that focus is. For example, a guided imagery meditation that relaxes you by focusing your imagination on the sights and sounds of the beach is compatible with Christian faith because it is connecting you with part of God's creation. But a mantra meditation in which you repeat words that contradict God's gospel truth would not be compatible.

6. *As a Christian, is it okay to use any kind of mindfulness meditation guides? There are a lot out there.*

It can be a little overwhelming to sort through the many mindfulness guides that are available. Sometimes meditations are labeled as "mindfulness" when they are really just meant to be calming, and this is not an accurate use of the term. Other times meditations are labeled as "Christian" but they are more filled with human distortions of faith rather than with God's truth.

You are encouraged to be discerning as you pick mindfulness meditation guides. Guides that are taken from Mindfulness-Based Stress Reduction (MBSR) or Mindfulness-Based Cognitive Therapy (MBCT) traditions are likely to be secular and grounded in research, with no specific mention of faith. These approaches are beneficial for your mental and physical health, and you can incorporate an awareness of God's presence throughout the practices if you choose. For a collection of guides that utilize MBSR and MBCT techniques that are explicitly blended with Christian faith, check out www.themindfulchristian.com.